Motherland

Mother land

A Jamaican Cookbook

Melissa Thompson

Interlink Books

An imprint of Interlink Publishing Group, Inc.
Northampton, Massachusetts

Contents

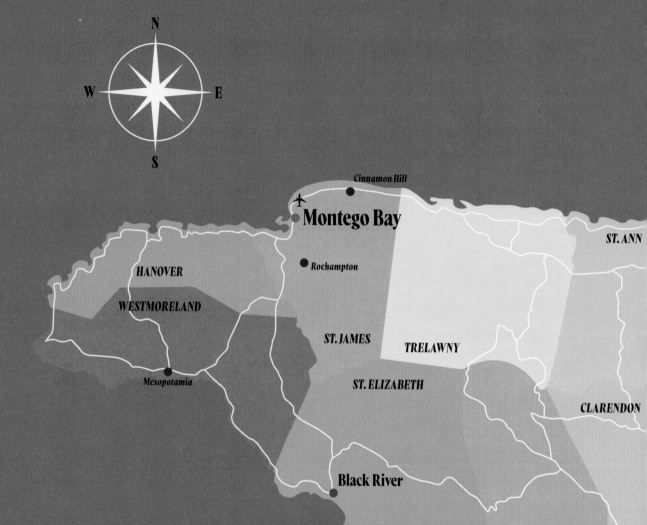

N
W E
S

Cinnamon Hill

Montego Bay

ST. ANN

Rochampton

HANOVER

WESTMORELAND

ST. JAMES

TRELAWNY

Mesopotamia

ST. ELIZABETH

CLARENDON

Black River

**CARIBBEAN
SEA**

Treasure Beach

MANCHESTER

KEY:
Capital
Major City
City/Place of Interest
Historical Place of Interest
REGION

CARIBBEAN
SEA

St. Ann's Bay

ST. MARY

Clarke Castle

Castleton

PORTLAND

Boston Beach

ST. CATHERINE

ST. ANDREW

BLUE MOUNTAINS

Kingston

Spanish Town

Caguaya Bay

Dalvey

ST. THOMAS

Jamaica
Yamaye / Xaymaca

Introduction

Standing in the kitchen of my childhood home, watching a pan of ackee and saltfish blipping away on the stove, my stomach rumbled with excitement.

I grew up in Weymouth, a seaside resort in Dorset on England's South Coast, where there were few Black people, let alone any Jamaican culture. Yet, in our kitchen at home, as I scooped up mouthfuls of my dad's famous ackee and saltfish with torn pieces of fried dumpling, or savored a slice of caramel-sweet plantain, if I closed my eyes, I could imagine I was in Jamaica. Each bite rooted me further to the island, a place where—at the time—I had never even been.

Back then, the only thing I really knew of my father's birthplace was gleaned from our atlas; Jamaica, measuring almost 150 miles (235 km) long and ranging from 21 miles (35 km) to 50 miles (82 km) wide, is the third biggest island in the Caribbean Sea, and lies South of Cuba and East of the Dominican Republic. The rest was conjured from Dad's descriptions of the food and the scenery of this tropical island, with its year-round warm weather, ample rainfall, and rich natural habitat for flourishing nature. He would tell us stories of how he climbed mango trees as a boy, sitting in their branches to feast on the sweet flesh until he woke up on the ground, having fallen asleep in a mango-induced slumber. Of his uncle sending him to dig up cassava from a nearby patch for dinner, or how he used to catch crayfish with his hands from the clear bubbling water of the stream that ran through the family's land.

Dad's parents, Altamont and Catherine, moved to Darlington in North East England in the mid 1950s. They were part of the "Windrush Generation," around 500,000 people who came to the UK from Caribbean islands between 1948-71, invited by the British government to help rebuild the country and boost the post-war labor shortage. The movement was named after the ship that brought the first group over, the HMT Empire Windrush.

Granddad worked as a bus driver. Alty, as he was known, and Catherine left Dad with his grandmother in Jamaica. He wouldn't see them again until he turned nine, when at last they could afford to send for him. Jamaica had been tough on Dad. He had no formal education, and, once his beloved grandmother died, he was left in the care of unkind relatives who made his life insufferable. Yet arriving in the UK was also a shock: the first time Dad had ever worn shoes was on his flight and he landed in England having lost one.

As a young man, Dad joined the Navy, and, while touring Malta, met my Maltese mom. After they got married, they settled by the English seaside. My brother was born, I followed three-and-a-half years later, and as for Mom and Dad, they both fed us the food they knew. Mom cooked us the Maltese pasta and soups she had grown up on. The Jamaican food from Dad was a salve for his homesickness, crucial familiarity in an unfamiliar world.

As a child, on cold rainy days, I would listen enraptured to Dad's tales of childhood in Jamaica. I would try and place myself in this country but, thousands of miles away, it couldn't feel more different. The descriptions of food always transported me best, bringing clarity in a way nothing else could. I did not realize it then, but I was doing what people have always done: using food as a ritual to connect to a place I missed. Even if, for me, I had never actually known the distant land I yearned for.

While we lacked a first-hand connection to his island, the food Dad made for us forged a link. I remember realising that what we cooked at home was different to the food my friends ate... and I couldn't help but feel they were missing out. Few Black people in Dorset, however, meant little to no provision for

these incredible Jamaican dishes. Occasionally, we'd travel to London to visit relatives and friends. On the way back we would stock up on all the foods and ingredients we couldn't get in Weymouth—goat meat, sugar cane, ginger beer, mangos, and plantain—and we'd cram the car trunk, ready to fill the freezer to see us through to our next visit.

Whenever we traveled to Darlington to visit Dad's parents, without fail Grandma would have a pot of her curry chicken on the stove. She always served it with rice and peas made with kidney beans, never gungo peas. Her curry was so good; I can still remember its peppery taste. It always made the six-hour drive to get there worth it.

During one visit, I asked Grandma to teach me how to make it. There were no measurements, just her innate understanding of when enough was enough. I committed Grandma's instructions to memory, determined to replicate this unbeatable meal. (I did, and you'll find the recipe here.)

At home, as soon as I was old enough, I was given small tasks to help out in the kitchen. I started out forming dumplings and peeling plantain, then, as I got older, I would cook the dishes I loved. Saltfish fritters, fried plantain, yam, patties, and that special curry chicken. After studying in London, when I moved back to Weymouth to work on the local paper, I would invite my friends over for vast pots of my curry goat.

Being a brown-skinned person in an almost entirely white area can foster a feeling of displacement, of not fitting in: I was looking for something, my roots, perhaps—anything—to hold on to. Cooking Jamaican food has always been a way for me to celebrate my heritage. But I realize now that it was also a way to create an anchor to Jamaica, just like my dad had done, just like countless people of the diaspora had done before us.

Dad had always been ambivalent about traveling back to his island, given his painful memories of growing up there, and we never pushed. In the absence of facts about my family tree, I filled in the gaps with the things I did know. It brought me comfort to think of my ancestors eating the same foods across the span of different generations and different continents. Our shared culinary history was—and remains—precious to me.

Then, in 2012, a last-minute change in travel plans saw us book a family vacation to the island, almost by accident. It was a fraught trip, as was to be expected for a journey with so much emotional baggage, but it was incredible. Stepping where my dad had last walked as a boy was incredibly powerful. And to finally eat the dishes I had grown up with, in their country of origin, was affirming. While researching this book in 2021, I went again, and my connection was only cemented. It felt like home.

Motherland is a recipe book, but more than that it is a history of the people, influences, and ingredients that uniquely united to create the wonderful patchwork cuisine that is Jamaican food today. Every dish and ingredient tells a story. And that context matters. From the Redware and Taíno peoples—the island's earliest known settlers—to the Spanish and British colonialists, to the enslaved African men and women brought to toil on the land, to the Indians, Chinese, and many other peoples who called the island home, everyone left their mark. But, without doubt, it was the men and women from Africa, who against their will came to the Caribbean islands during the transatlantic slave trade, that had the biggest influence on the island's food and culture. This barbaric industry changed the face of Jamaica forever: its population, language, music, and landscape, as well as its food. The cuisine is a beautiful product of this violent chapter in world history.

While nose-to-tail eating has only been embraced relatively recently in the West by the middle classes, for Jamaicans it has been part of the culinary armory for centuries. Often, enslaved men, women, and children were given offcuts the white slavers had no desire for and such was their resourcefulness that little was wasted. They brought with them their one-pot cooking traditions, so dishes such as cow foot soup, mannish water, and red peas soup were born, along with more substantial hotpot recipes such as stewed oxtail and brown stew chicken.

Today, more than ninety percent of Jamaicans are descended from West and Central African people who were enslaved. And somewhere within that horrific system were my ancestors. I know nothing of them and I struggle to think of the suffering they must have endured. Though I am thankful they survived to have families, I can only hope that their children, my great-great-great-grandmother and grandfather, were created out of love.

Motherland includes many of the familiar Jamaican dishes we cooked in my family, as well as some of my own recipes, rooted in the island's ingredients. After all, food is constantly evolving. This is by no means intended to be the definitive book on Jamaica's food, in fact a couple of important national dishes are notable for their absence, such as mannish water and chicken foot soup. I decided not to include those simply because they are not a regular feature of my kitchen repertoire. Rather, I like to think that this book is a good starting point from which to explore, experiment, and enjoy.

The island's motto is "Out of Many, One People." That sentiment goes for the food too. Jamaica's food sits side-by-side with its past, an edible timeline of its story and a tangible expression of the mood and circumstances of each moment. Whether created through nostalgia or necessity, the island's cooking is the legacy of every chapter in its history. To me it is one of the finest—and most singular—cuisines in the world.

Above all, I hope my book is a tribute to the people whose strength and resilience saw them go much further when cooking for their families than simply to provide sustenance; instead they strove to create—and succeeded in sparking—culinary magic, its longevity testament to their skill.

Humans have always used food as a connection to the place that they or their ancestors came from. This is partly functional: you cook what you know. But it is also a vital source of comfort. It is this desire to connect, to comfort, and to remember that lies at the heart of Jamaican cuisine.

It is a way of telling our story without uttering a word.

Snacks

They may be little, but Jamaican snacks pack in a lot. An island of busy people needs substantial bites to sustain them as they go about their business.

These mighty mouthfuls are arrestingly delicious. That first bite of a patty, filled with steaming-hot spiced lamb that begs to be allowed to cool down before you dig in... but always proves too tempting, as burnt lips testify. Saltfish fritters, so delicious that you can't help reaching out for another even though you already have one in the other hand. Salads and small bites that lift a main dish, or are a meal in their own right.

Cook several at a time and enjoy them as a feast together; ingredients grown alongside one another bringing harmony to each plate.

The Jamaican flavors, the island memories, the always wanting more.

A roadside food stall in Manchester

STAMP & GO (SALTFISH FRITTERS)

These have to be one of the most addictive snacks known to humankind. Salty and slightly spicy, a bit crispy yet soft inside, they check all the boxes, but are really easy to make. The best I've ever had are made by my auntie Dianne, and luckily she makes loads when she cooks a batch. Thankfully, these measure up pretty well too.

According to the *Jamaica Observer* newspaper, they get their name from a saying of British naval officers of the 18th century who, if they wanted something done quickly, would bark: "Stamp and go."

SERVES 4 AS A LIGHT MEAL

9 oz (250 g) saltfish
½ red onion, finely chopped
3 scallions, finely chopped
½ red or orange pepper, finely chopped
2⅓ cups (280 g) all-purpose flour
1¼ cups (300 ml) water
oil, for frying (use a flavorless oil such as vegetable, sunflower, or canola)
sea salt and freshly ground black pepper
lime wedges, to serve

Rinse the saltfish under plenty of water and then soak it overnight in a large container that will fit in your fridge. Change the water at least twice while it soaks.

Boil the saltfish in a pan of fresh water until cooked through, about 5 minutes. Leave to cool, then flake into a mixing bowl, checking for bones and removing them along with the skin as you go.

Add the red onion and scallions to the bowl, with the red or orange pepper and a pinch of black pepper. Don't add salt yet.

Tip in the flour, then pour in the measured water a bit at a time, stirring between additions. You want the mixture to be thick so it falls off a wooden spoon in lumps rather than in a continuous stream of batter. Take a spoon and taste a tiny amount to check for seasoning, adding a pinch of salt if needed.

Pour oil into a large frying pan so it's ¼ in (5 mm) deep and heat it over medium to medium-high heat. Spoon about 2 tablespoons of mixture into the oil to form a fritter. Add another 2–3 fritters, depending on the size of your pan, but do not overcrowd the pan. Cook for 3 minutes until firm, then turn and cook for another 3 minutes. Turn again and cook until golden brown, a further 2 minutes, then repeat until both sides are golden brown.

Remove from the oil and transfer to a plate lined with paper towels. Serve immediately with lime wedges, while you cook the remaining fritters.

CURRY LAMB PATTIES

Patty shops abound in Jamaica and I cannot pass one without stopping for a couple. They differ wildly from shop to shop: some have flaky pastry, others shortcrust; some are the color of sand, others are dyed the trademark "patty yellow," a color achieved through the use of turmeric or annatto.

And they come in myriad flavors. My favorite is lamb, but there are also vegetable, beef and cheese, callaloo and saltfish (see overleaf), chicken. . . the list is endless.

I like the pastry for my patties to be short and crumbly, so that is the result you will get with this recipe. It may be more difficult to work with, but stick with it and the results are worth it.

MAKES 8-10

For the pastry
1 tbsp ground annatto or ground turmeric
2 tbsp vegetable oil (optional)
3¾ cups (450 g) all-purpose flour
1½ tsp Jamaican curry powder
 (for homemade, see page 23)
1 tsp sea salt
1 cup (180 g) chilled white vegetable fat /
 shortening
5 tbsp (75 g) chilled unsalted butter
1½ tbsp apple cider vinegar
scant 1 cup (200-225 ml) ice-cold water
1 egg, lightly beaten

For the filling
14 oz (400 g) ground lamb
1 onion, finely chopped
½ red bell pepper, finely chopped
1 garlic clove, crushed
1½ tbsp Jamaican curry powder
 (for homemade, see page 23)
1 tsp freshly ground black pepper
1 cup (250 ml) lamb stock or chicken stock
 (for homemade, see page 138)

If using annatto, steep it in the 2 tablespoons oil in a saucepan over medium-low heat until the oil has turned orange, 10–15 minutes. Drain through a small sieve into a bowl, scraping the pan of as much oil as you can.

To make the pastry, mix the flour, annatto oil or turmeric, curry powder, and salt in a bowl and grate in the chilled shortening and butter. Handling the mixture as little as possible, move it around to coat the fat in flour, then tip it all into a food processor. Pulse until the mixture resembles breadcrumbs, adding the vinegar, then gradually pour in enough of the measured ice-cold water until the dough comes together. Wrap it in plastic wrap or wax paper and refrigerate.

Meanwhile, fry the lamb in a dry frying pan, breaking it up with a wooden spoon, until browned all over, then add the onion, red pepper, garlic, curry powder, black pepper, and salt to taste. Cook for 10 minutes, then pour in the stock and cook for another 10 minutes. Remove from the heat and cool completely.

Preheat the oven to 350°F (180°C).

Roll the pastry out so it's ⅛ in (2 mm) thick, protecting your work surface with a piece of parchment paper to stop it from being dyed yellow. Using a bowl or a plate about 6 in (16 cm) in diameter as a guide, cut circles out of the pastry, spacing them to get as many out of the pastry as possible. (You can re-roll the offcuts once.)

Spoon 2 tablespoons of the cold meat filling on to half of a pastry circle, leaving a 1 in (2.5 cm) border around the edge. Brush the edge with egg, fold the pastry over, and press to secure. Then use the tines of a fork to press down around the full curved edge of the semi-circle. Repeat to fill and form all the patties.

Brush the top of the patties with more egg, pierce with a fork, then bake for 25 minutes. Leave to cool for 15 minutes before enjoying.

CALLALOO & SALTFISH PATTIES

Saltfish and callaloo works really well as a patty and dumpling (see page 48) filling (I buy callaloo and saltfish stuffed dumpling whenever I'm in Brixton, South London, where there is a large Jamaican population, and it's so good). Lighter than meat versions, this patty is still packed with flavor and is quick and easy to make, once you've soaked the saltfish.

MAKES 8–10

9 oz (250 g) saltfish, rinsed and soaked
    overnight (see page 18)
1 tbsp vegetable oil
½ onion, finely sliced
1 tomato, finely chopped
1 red bell pepper, finely chopped
2 scallions, finely chopped
2 garlic cloves, crushed
leaves from 4 thyme sprigs
¼–½ Scotch bonnet, finely chopped,
    to taste (optional)
1 big bunch of callaloo (bunched mature
    spinach or Tuscan kale work well too),
    coarse stalks removed, chopped
1 quantity patty Pastry (see page 21)
1 egg, lightly beaten
freshly ground black pepper

Cook the saltfish and remove the skin and bones (see page 18).

Put the oil in a frying pan over medium heat and cook the onion for 8 minutes until soft. Add the tomato, red pepper, scallions, garlic, thyme, a pinch of black pepper, and the Scotch bonnet, if using. Cook for 8 minutes, adding a splash of water if the pan seems dry.

Add the saltfish and callaloo and cook for another 5 minutes, until the sauce has reduced and the greens are soft. Taste for seasoning and add salt if needed.

Form the patties with the pastry and egg and bake as on page 21.

JAMAICAN CURRY POWDER

This is the spice blend I use for Curry Goat, Grandma's Curry Chicken, and Curry Fried Chicken (see pages 168, 135, and 142), as well as for many other Jamaican dishes such as my patties (see opposite and page 21). You can use a pre-made curry powder too, that's fine; I'd go for a Madras variety and add a bit of extra ground turmeric. But it's always pleasing to put together your own, and it's really easy.

Not many spices are native to Jamaica, save for pimento (allspice) and perhaps a type of bay. The majority of other spices in the food were brought to the island aboard ships, either those of the early colonialists during the transatlantic trade, or those of buccaneers after looting enemy vessels. Their use became more widespread thanks to a wave of immigration from India through indentured servitude.

MAKES ABOUT 3½ OZ (100 G)

1 tbsp coriander seeds
1 tbsp cumin seeds
½ tbsp dried pimento (allspice) berries
½ tbsp fenugreek seeds
1 tsp cloves
1 tsp paprika
2 tbsp ground turmeric

Mix all the spices together and store in an airtight container for up to 3 months.

Shake before use, remove as much as you need, then grind it to a powder. Keeping the spices whole will help it to remain fresh and aromatic.

MANGO & GRAPEFRUIT SALAD

Mango and grapefruit are often used in sweet dishes, but I love them with savory food. This salad shows them off at their best and the sweet mango and tart grapefruit make it a perfect accompaniment to meat and fish, especially those that have a bit of chile heat.

SERVES 4 AS A SIDE

finely grated zest and juice of 2 limes
2 tbsp canola or olive oil
½ Scotch bonnet, deseeded and very
    finely chopped (optional)
½ red onion, finely sliced and rinsed
    with water
1 Little Gem lettuce, leaves separated and
    roughly chopped
1 grapefruit, segments cut out of their skins
2 ripe mangos, peeled and finely sliced
1 scallion, finely sliced
sea salt and freshly ground black pepper

Mix together the lime zest and juice, oil, Scotch bonnet, if using, red onion, and a pinch each of salt and pepper.

Now turn the lettuce leaves with this dressing and scatter them on a plate. Lay the grapefruit and mangos on top and gently mix through the leaves.

Sprinkle with the scallion and serve.

CRISPY SPICED BUTTER BEANS

Beans grow abundantly in Jamaica and have been a great source of protein for hundreds of years. That they dry and keep for ages is an added bonus. I've found that some butter beans take longer than others to cook, so do keep an eye on them and be patient to get that unmistakable crisp. Keep mixing them around in the oil too, so that when they split the interior gets coated; that's the secret to getting them crispy.

These are a quick, easy snack that you can mix up as you choose. I like to go heavy with the spice mix.

SERVES 4-6 AS A SNACK

14 oz (400 g) can of butter beans, drained
1 tsp smoked paprika
½ tsp onion powder
½ tsp ground ginger
1 tsp freshly ground black pepper
½ tsp ground pimento (allspice)
½ tsp sea salt
1 tbsp olive oil

Preheat the oven to 350°F (180°C).

Spread the beans on a baking sheet lined with parchment paper. Pierce each one with a toothpick and place in the oven for 10 minutes to dry them out.

Mix the spices and salt together in a small bowl.

Mix the butter beans with the oil, then sprinkle over the spice mix, and shake to cover all the beans.

Reduce the oven temperature to 320°F (160°C) and roast the butter beans for 40-60 minutes until they are crispy. Mix them during the cooking to coat the inside of any bean that has burst open with the spiced oil, to ensure they become crispy on the inside, or else they will be floury.

TOASTED CORN FRITTERS

Corn fritters are one of my most favorite things. With an egg and a side of avocado salsa, they make the best breakfast. Apart from ackee and saltfish, of course.

A few years ago, I experimented with browning corn in butter before adding it to fritters. It gives a lovely, subtly toasted corn flavor that reminds me almost of popcorn. It's a little extra effort, but one that's worth it, I think.

SERVES 4–6 AS A LIGHT MEAL

1¼ cups (150 g) all-purpose flour
1½ tsp baking powder
1 egg, lightly beaten
⅔ cup (150 ml) milk
1⅓ cups (200 g) corn kernels
5 tbsp (75 g) unsalted butter
½ red onion, finely chopped
3 scallions, finely chopped
½ red bell pepper, finely chopped
½ yellow bell pepper, finely chopped
1 tsp sea salt
1 tsp freshly ground black pepper
vegetable oil, for frying

To serve
Avocado Salsa (see page 30)
poached eggs

Mix the flour, baking powder, egg, and milk together to form a stiff batter. Leave to rest while you prepare the rest of the ingredients.

Toast the corn kernels in a dry pan for a few minutes over medium heat, then add the butter. Fry until the kernels start to brown and the butter begins to smell nutty. Remove from the heat.

Mix the onion, scallions, and red and yellow peppers into the batter along with the toasted corn and season with the salt and pepper.

Add enough oil to a deep frying pan so it's 1 in (2.5 cm) deep and heat over medium heat until a piece of batter dropped into it will sink and then rise, bubbling after a couple of seconds.

Scoop a heaped tablespoon of batter and drop into the oil, then another, working in a clockwise direction round the edge of the pan and not overcrowding it.

Cook for 4 minutes, then turn in the order they were added and cook for another 3 or so minutes. Remove the fritters, again in the order they were added, and place on a wire rack with paper towels underneath to soak up the oil.

Repeat until all the batter is used up. You may need to add a bit more oil.

Serve with Avocado Salsa and poached eggs.

MANGO & LIME SALSA

Great with chicken wings, fish, or anything fried. It's fresh and zingy, so really livens up whatever it's served with.

SERVES 4

2 semi-firm mangos, peeled and
   finely chopped
finely grated zest and juice of 1 lime
½ Scotch bonnet, deseeded and
   finely chopped
pinch of sea salt

Mix all the ingredients together and serve.

AVOCADO SALSA

A refreshing, delicious side to many seafood or vegetable dishes, especially to Toasted Corn Fritters and Pressed Plantain (see pages 28 and 215), this is quick and easy to make. It won't keep for long, but one thing you can do to stop it oxidizing and going brown is to get a damp piece of paper towel and lay it on top of the salsa, so it is making contact. Then place the covered bowl in a sealed container and it should last for at least 6 hours.

SERVES 4

3 ripe avocados
2 scallions, finely sliced
2 tomatoes, deseeded and chopped
¼ Scotch bonnet, deseeded and
   finely chopped
finely grated zest and juice of 2 limes
sea salt and freshly ground black pepper

Peel, pit, and chop the avocados into small pieces. Mix with the scallions, tomatoes, Scotch bonnet, and lime zest and juice.

Season to taste and mix gently, being careful not to mash the salsa.

CASSAVA FRITTERS

The versatility of cassava is boundless and these fritters are a brilliant way to enjoy it without the labor-intensive preparation involved in making Bammy (see page 197).

    The first cassava fritters I ate were at Chishuru, a Nigerian restaurant in Brixton, in South London, run by my friend Joké Bakare. These are inspired by hers, though they are quite different. You can make a big batch of these and freeze them. I love them with a hearty cooked breakfast.

SERVES 4-6 AS A SNACK

1 lb 5 oz (600 g) peeled and grated cassava
1 egg, lightly beaten
1 tsp sea salt
1 tsp smoked paprika
1 tsp thyme leaves
vegetable oil and unsalted butter,
    for cooking
Pepper Sauce Mayo, to serve (optional,
    see page 47)

Squeeze the grated cassava gently to remove most of the liquid, but not all. Mix it in a bowl with the egg, salt, paprika, and thyme and set aside for 10 minutes.

Heat some oil and 1 teaspoon butter in a frying pan over medium heat. Add a ball of cassava batter the size of a small plum to the oil and press it down lightly with a spatula. Repeat, going around the edge of the pan, and fry for 6–7 minutes until golden brown. Flip the fritters in the order they were added and fry until the other side is golden brown and they are completely cooked through. (Because of the potential toxicity of the cassava, it's important to cook it thoroughly to kill any of the toxin.) Add more oil and butter if needed.

Remove, place between sheets of paper towels and gently squeeze to absorb as much of the oil as possible, then transfer to a wire rack while you cook the remaining fritters. Serve with a cooked breakfast, or with Pepper Sauce Mayo as a snack.

A shady glade in St. Mary

Columbus: Myth & Murder

When I was growing up in 1980s Britain, we were taught that Christopher Columbus was an intrepid explorer who "discovered" the Americas. That's not the way it was seen in my house, though. If Dad heard the 15th-century navigator described that way, he would tut and shake his head. I knew what was coming next.

"'Discover?" he would repeat, exasperated. "How can you 'discover' somewhere if people are already living there?"

I never really understood why it annoyed him so much. To everyone else, it seemed, Columbus was a hero. What was Dad's problem?

As I got older, and learned more about the history of Jamaica and the rest of the Caribbean, I understood Dad's frustration. Columbus did not "discover" anything; others had beaten him to it. By millennia, actually. The "New World" was not new to them, in fact it had been their world for a thousand years. And while Columbus may well have been a good navigator and an intuitive explorer, he was a weak and poor leader, desperate for glory.

His greed and vicious disregard for anyone who threatened to get in the way of his ambition led to the near-total genocide of the indigenous population across vast swathes of the Caribbean islands, in the cruellest manner.

A popular narrative in the West is that most of the indigenous Caribbean population were killed by new diseases introduced by the Europeans, against which they had little immunity. While that did indeed happen to an extent, most were in fact murdered, either directly through mindless violence, or indirectly through starvation, or by being worked to their deaths. Within fifty years of Europe's colonization of the islands, hundreds of thousands of men, women, and children perished throughout the Caribbean.

And the violence did not stop there. The European invaders, those righteous Christian men who proclaimed moral superiority over the islanders, routinely raped the indigenous women and girls.

Those early colonizers laid the foundation for the slave societies later built by the British and other European states across the Caribbean and South America. Thanks to stolen free labor, the colonizers accrued incredible wealth—a vital step towards funding the Industrial Revolution in the UK—while the societies they plundered were left destitute and their people uprooted.

In the Beginning

The island's first known inhabitants, 500–650 CE, were from the Ostionoid culture, sometimes referred to as Redware people after the red-slipped pottery they left behind. They originated in South America and were pioneers, thought to have migrated through the Caribbean islands before making Jamaica their home. The Taíno emerged from the same migratory pattern and had genetic links to the Arawaks of South America, even speaking a similar language.

The Taíno—an Arawak word believed to mean "good man," to differentiate them from the feared Guanahatebeys and Kalinago, or Island Caribs—made up the largest indigenous group in the Caribbean. They did not have a written language, so almost all we know of them comes from records made by the first Spaniards who arrived in the Caribbean islands at the end of the 15th century.

And because the Taíno were almost entirely wiped out in the Spanish genocide, their culture mostly died along with them, though some did survive, and there are Jamaicans today who believe they are descended from Taíno.

The Taíno were thriving before the colonizers arrived. Contemporaneous records suggest the most populous islands at the time of European contact— Puerto Rico and Hispaniola especially—had "millions" of people living on them, though today this is believed to have been an exaggeration. Modern estimates put the Taíno population in Jamaica at a more modest 100,000.

The region's geography meant that some islands were visible to each other, allowing relatively easy trading. They used canoes made from single tree trunks, often beautifully decorated. However, not all the different tribes got along: the Kalinago, for instance, were believed to raid islands looking for women to take as "wives." The Europeans alleged that the Kalinago also practiced cannibalism, though this is disputed; some historians think it more likely that Europeans used the charge as justification for their violence against them.

The Taíno were described as light-skinned, but are thought to have often painted themselves different colors, including red using annatto seeds, the same seeds originally used to color patty pastry its trademark yellow-orange (see page 21). This practice perhaps gave rise to the common depiction of "red-skinned" indigenous Americans. They wore nothing, apart from small decorative pieces of cloth. Early European records portray the Taíno as generous and kind-hearted; belongings were seen as communal, so sharing was automatic. They enjoyed sports, including batey, a game played with a rubber ball on specially built courts which also served as the stage for group entertainments such as singing and dancing. The Taíno were exquisite wood carvers, none more so than in Jamaica, whose woodcraft was said to be the finest of all the islands.

The Caribbean Taíno people created a well-structured, prosperous agricultural two-class society, consisting of nobility and ordinary working folk. They lived in villages, each ruled by a *cacique* (chief), under larger chiefdoms ruled by overarching *caciques*. The authority of the *caciques* was unquestioned. They governed society, allocating roles and responsibilities to the village people. They also meted out punishments: theft was punishable by death. Before long, the Redware people were incorporated into the burgeoning Taíno population, though whether through subjugation or a gradual assimilation is unknown.

In his *Historia de las Indias*, a three-volume tome written between 1527 and 1561, Bartolomé de las Casas, a friar and anti-slavery campaigner who was on Christopher Columbus's third voyage, described large communal bell-shaped residences, made of wood and roofed with palm leaves, some housing as many as six hundred people. Inside, the Taíno slept on hammocks—a word we get from the Arawak *hamoca*—though *caciques* sometimes slept on raised wooden platforms.

The Taíno thrived on the island's bountiful resources, fishing extensively and planting maize, sweet potato, and—most importantly—cassava, a key ingredient upon which Jamaica was arguably built. They were efficient farmers who used the conuco system of cultivation: little mounds of soil that enabled the roots to spread out and did not require much water or earth. It is a system still in use today.

First Contact

It was the Taíno who greeted the Spanish fleet led by Columbus when it reached the Caribbean islands in October 1492.

Italian-born Columbus had been determined to find a westward route from Europe to Asia. Unable to reach India, China, Japan, or the fabled "Spice Islands of Asia" via the coast of Africa—because the Ottoman Empire controlled those waters, and the overground routes were blocked too—Columbus was convinced that a direct route across the Atlantic was not only possible, and quicker, but also lucrative. If he succeeded, the subsequent expansion of the Spanish empire would bring him and his sponsors unimaginable wealth in the gold, pearls, precious stones, spices, and other treasures of those lands.

As a crusader, Columbus also sought to bring Christianity to the East. The King and Queen of Spain, Ferdinand and Isabella, agreed to fund the trip after rejecting him at least twice, and, in August 1492, the fleet—Pinta, Niña, and Columbus's favorite and largest of the three, the flagship Santa María—set sail from Palos de la Frontera in Spain, destined for the "Indies." Little did he know that the Americas, a continent hitherto unknown to Europeans, would get in his way.

The voyage was long and arduous. Barely a month in, the crew were growing increasingly ill-tempered and impatient. Their hostility festered amid false sightings of land, as they began to doubt their captain's navigational skills. Furious, they questioned if they should either "rid him out the way or else to caste him into the sea." But Columbus persisted, reassuring the crew and promising them that they were close to their goal.

In October 1492, two months after they set sail, they spotted land for the first time: Guanahani, in the Bahamas. Columbus renamed it San Salvador, which remains its name. The islanders rowed out to greet the Spanish fleet in canoes. They must have been stunned at the sight of these strange men in European clothing, their exotic sails billowing atop the enormous three-masted vessels.

Columbus was charmed by the good nature and generosity of this welcoming party. He named them "Indians," believing he had reached the "Indies" (the Far East). They exchanged gifts and the *caciques* greeted the incomers warmly. But beneath the Spaniards' broad smiles, they were already sizing the Taíno up for their own gain. Shortly after his arrival, Columbus wrote in his journal:

> "They all go naked as their mothers bore them... They are very well built, with very handsome bodies, and very good countenances... They should be good servants and intelligent... and I believe that they would easily be made Christians."

The Spaniards continued their explorations of the Caribbean islands, claiming and renaming some as they went, despite the fact they already had names. (Jamaica and Cuba retained their names.) Interactions between the Taíno and the Spaniards were initially good natured. Columbus wrote that he and his officers took pains to be on their best behavior with the Taíno,

> "In order that they should hold us in this esteem and that another time when your Highnesses send here again they may not receive your people badly."

His main priority, though, was finding gold. Noticing flashes of the precious metal in jewelry worn by the *caciques*, he asked where they got it from. Initially he was told more could be found in Haiti, which was then the name for the whole island, half of which is now called the Dominican Republic. So that is where the fleet headed next.

A hill in St. Mary, seen from the road to Portland

The Haitian Taíno fled the Spaniards at first, fearing the sight of the strangers. But, eventually, the islanders warmed to the Europeans and shared food and gifts with them. They traded gold, although it transpired that the precious metal was not as abundant as Columbus had hoped; what little there was required laborious sifting to glean very small amounts, which was then beaten into sheets.

The Spaniards sailed around the island's coast, intermittently going ashore and investigating, but in December 1492 the Santa María ran aground and could not be saved. Thanks to the Taíno, who salvaged everything with canoes, all the crew and their belongings were rescued.

Although devastated at the loss of his flagship, Columbus came to believe the accident was due to divine intervention, a sign that they should make their first settlement on Haiti, which he renamed "La Isla Española," or, in Latin, "Hispaniola." When the fleet sailed home to Spain, thirty-nine willing volunteers remained, along with enough supplies to last a year. They built a fort out of salvaged wood from the Santa María, calling the settlement *La Navidad*: "birth."

In March 1493, Columbus arrived back in Spain to a hero's welcome. He was made an Admiral of the Ocean and no expense was spared in preparing for his return to the Caribbean to continue the region's colonization. Importantly, Columbus was also granted a ten percent stake in any riches to be gleaned from this new territory, be they gold, spices, or gems.

Seventeen ships were made ready, packed with more than one thousand men, including miners, carpenters, blacksmiths, and horsemen. They took livestock—cattle, sheep, goats, and pigs—and crop foods to sow, such as wheat, barley, peas and corn, grape vines, and fruit trees including bananas and citrus. This was also the first time sugar cane was introduced to the Caribbean.

Back in the Caribbean in November 1493, the Spaniards arrived once more at the La Navidad settlement in Hispaniola. What greeted them was a disaster. The wooden fortress had been burned to the ground and all the Spanish settlers were dead. Guacanagari, a *cacique* whom Columbus had befriended, said that they had been killed by a rival chief in retaliation for the Spaniards' ill treatment of the Taíno, notably the rape of the women and violence against the men. Columbus ordered a new settlement to be built on the western side of the island, called La Isabela after the Spanish Queen, and resumed his exploration of the Caribbean.

After Columbus's departure, however, the Isabela settlement soon went into rapid decline. Many Spaniards fell sick and died. Having torn through their own resources, they became dependent on the food, particularly sweet potato and cassava, obtained through trade with the Taíno, whom they soon placed under brutal subjugation. They introduced a tribute system whereby the Taíno had to fulfil targets of gold and provisions for the Spaniards, or be punished. Their demands were so cripplingly punitive that the Taíno had to neglect their own crops to meet them, which likely caused a famine in 1495 that lasted two years. In Spain, reports about the chaos unfolding in the new colony showed Columbus in a very poor light. Eventually he had to return to Spain to answer his critics, leaving his brother Bartolomé in charge.

In 1498, Columbus mounted a third voyage to Hispaniola but, two years later, the Spaniards sent an investigator to the island, who was horrified by what he saw there. Columbus and his brother were arrested and sent back to Spain in chains. However, it was not the treatment of the Taíno that was the cause of European disgust, but rather the chaos among the Spaniards; many had returned home, others had died, and by 1500, just a few hundred remained on Hispaniola.

Xaymaca

Still Columbus held out hopes of untold riches, which spurred him on to make a fourth and final voyage. He had another island in his sights, one which the Taíno told him was rich with gold. It was called Yamaye, or Xaymaca, an island Columbus had first sighted in 1494 but was yet to explore.

By the time Columbus finally made it back to the Caribbean, it was early 1503 and his reputation was in tatters. Banned from Hispaniola, his fleet moved around until more than a dozen ships foundered in a storm with the loss of many men. Columbus was shipwrecked off the North of Xaymaca, near modern-day St. Ann's Bay, his boat too battered and worm-eaten to continue.

A small group of his crew ventured inland to make contact with the local Taíno, exchanging beads and trinkets for food. Before long, though, the goodwill of the islanders was exhausted. They complained that "one Christian eats as much as twenty of them" and refused to give the Spaniards any more food.

To counter this, Columbus had a trick up his sleeve. A ship's almanac predicted that a solar eclipse was to take place in the coming days. Columbus told the Taíno that his Christian God was angry with them for their lack of generosity and would smite them with pestilence and famine unless they relented.

> "... As a sign of the truth of it, next night they should see the Moon eclipsed. The Indians brought him Victuals, when they saw the Prediction fulfill'd. He liv'd by the effects of this Eclipse till Boats came from Hispaniola, and carried him and his Men thither!"

Columbus remained in Jamaica for a year before he was rescued. He then made his final voyage home to Spain. He died two years later, in relative obscurity, still believing he had, in fact, discovered the Indies.

In 1509 Columbus's son, Diego, was made Viceroy of the Indies and colonized Jamaica that same year. The first settlement, Sevilla la Nueva, was built on the North Coast, close to where Columbus had been shipwrecked, in modern-day St. Ann's Bay. The site was abandoned in about 1524 and a new town, Villa de la Vega, was built where Spanish Town stands today. There are few records about the early days of Jamaican colonization, but a letter from the Spanish court in 1511 commanded the colonizers that "the Indians shall not bear burdens or be subjected to other injurious treatment such as was used in the past at Hispaniola." But they paid little heed. The writing was on the wall for the Jamaican Taíno, whose population had already dwindled drastically. Most Taíno men were set to work in agriculture, growing cotton, tobacco, and other crops to fuel the Spanish empire, but some were forced into labor, building roads. The women were tasked with making items out of the cotton, including hammocks and clothing.

According to Bartolomé de las Casas, who reported from Hispaniola in 1502, Spanish settlers had become so lazy that they would ride Taíno like horses. Others they treated like donkeys, ordering them to carry heavy loads. De las Casas's writings are full of devastating descriptions of the Spaniards' bloodlust. Once, he wrote, some Spanish men stopped two boys who were carrying parrots. They stole the birds... and decapitated the boys for fun. He noted:

> "It was a general rule among Spaniards to be cruel; not just cruel but extraordinarily cruel so that harsh and bitter treatment would prevent Indians from daring to think of themselves as human beings."

Illness accounted for many deaths among the Taíno, too. Rolling outbreaks of influenza, smallpox, and other diseases took a heavy toll on both the Taíno and the Spaniards who had brought the diseases with them to the Caribbean.

Although there is little consensus about how many Taíno people lived in the Caribbean at the time of European contact, the decimation of their numbers because of the Spanish presence is inarguable. One estimate states that out of the suggested population of 300,000–600,000 at the time of Columbus's landing in 1492, by 1512—a mere twenty years later—just 20,000 remained. By the 1550s, there were barely any surviving Taíno on Hispaniola.

With such a diminished workforce, the Caribbean became a backwater to the Spaniards. Over time, the animals they had brought became wild and multiplied, while the fruits and vegetables imported on Spanish ships flourished in the fertile soil across the island. Gradually, many Spaniards returned to Spain; others made for Cuba or South America to seek their fortune. Those that stayed concentrated their efforts on less labor-intensive livestock farming. For what labor they did need, now the Taíno were decimated, they turned to other Caribbean islands, to South America. . . and eventually to Africa.

In Jamaica, the export of horses, beef, and pork products became the main source of income. Eighty thousand pigs were killed for their lard in one year alone. The lard was shipped out of Montego Bay, which is said to have got its name from its 16th-century title *Bahia De Mantega*, meaning "Bay of Lard." But despite the huge impact sugar was later to have on the region, the Spaniards didn't focus on Jamaica as a prime spot for sugar cane cultivation.

The English, on the other hand, had the island in their sights. In 1655, the major European powers—Spain, Portugal, Netherlands, France, and England—were on a frenzied mission to conquer the New World. England, under Oliver Cromwell, was at war with Spain, locked in a battle of bitter commercial rivalry. As each side attacked the other's commercial and colonial interests, Cromwell's fleet set sail for the Caribbean Sea.

Continued on page 63

The Portland coastline

OXTAIL NUGGETS WITH PEPPER SAUCE MAYO

I once made these with leftovers and my partner Kate insisted I put the recipe in the book: she loves them. If "leftover oxtail" seems like an impossible dream, bear with me. I've devised my recipe for Stewed Oxtail (see page 167) to make enough to provide leftovers, considering how rich and satisfying it is.

As these are such an excellent snack, they're also worth making just for their own sake. Sure, they're labor intensive, but they're well worth it.

SERVES 4–6 AS A SNACK

about 14 oz (400 g) leftover Stewed Oxtail
   (see page 167)
⅔ cup (80 g) all-purpose flour
1 egg, lightly beaten
1⅔ cups (80 g) panko breadcrumbs
vegetable oil, for deep-frying
1 scallion, finely sliced

For the Pepper Sauce Mayo
4 tbsp mayonnaise
1 tbsp Pepper Sauce (see page 278)

While the oxtail is still warm, clean the meat from the bones and shred the meat. Find a square or rectangular plastic container big enough so that when the oxtail is added it sits about ¾ in (2 cm) deep. Press the oxtail and its sauce down in the container as firmly as possible, ensuring you flatten it and leave no holes or gaps. Refrigerate for at least 4 hours, until it is solid.

Set up 3 bowls, fill the first with the flour, the second with the egg, and the last with the panko crumbs.

Remove the oxtail from the fridge and turn it out on to a chopping board, being careful not to break it. Mark the oxtail block into squares; the size will depend on its dimensions, but try to get ¾ in (2 cm) cubes. Cut them out. Now first place a cube into the flour and carefully ensure it's covered, then into the egg, and finally into the crumbs. Place on a plate while you repeat to coat the rest of the cubes.

Following all the usual precautions for deep-frying (see page 288), heat oil in a pot to 350°F (180°C) and fry the nuggets for 4 minutes, turning, until golden and crispy on all sides. Remove and drain on a wire rack. Place some paper towels under the rack to soak up any oil, but don't drain the nuggets directly on the paper towels, or they won't crisp up properly.

Combine the mayonnaise with the Pepper Sauce and serve with the nuggets, sprinkled with the scallion.

STUFFED DUMPLING WITH CALLALOO & SALTFISH

Brixton in South London became a hub for Jamaicans during the post-war period, when people from Jamaica and across the British colonies of the Caribbean moved to Britain as part of the Windrush Generation. As it was a working-class area, the new arrivals were able to find affordable lodging there, unlike in other areas of the capital, where they were kept out by racist lodging policies. And although Brixton has become gentrified, as has much of London, it just about retains its Caribbean heart.

One of my favorite spots is First Choice Bakers on Atlantic Road. They do amazing bun, great hard dough bread and, my absolute favorite, fried dumpling stuffed with callaloo and saltfish. This recipe is in honor of them, and for my happy memories of stopping there for snacks. The dumpling is pretty much the same recipe as my Fried Dumpling (see page 224), but is worth giving in full here, as it is shaped and cooked in a different way.

SERVES 6 AS A LIGHT MEAL

For the dumplings
3 cups (350 g) all-purpose flour
⅓ cup (50 g) fine cornmeal
1½ tsp baking powder
1 tsp sugar
3½ tbsp milk
about 3½ tbsp water
vegetable oil, for deep-frying
pinch of sea salt
hot sauce, to serve (optional)

For the filling
1 tbsp vegetable oil
½ onion, sliced
1 red bell pepper, chopped
1 tomato, chopped
2 scallions, chopped
2 garlic cloves, crushed
leaves from 4 thyme sprigs
1 Scotch bonnet (optional)
9 oz (250 g) saltfish, rinsed and soaked overnight (see page 18)
1 big bunch of callaloo (bunched mature spinach or Tuscan kale work well too), coarse stalks removed, chopped
sea salt and freshly ground black pepper

Mix the flour, cornmeal, baking powder, sugar, and salt in a bowl. Gradually add the milk, then splash in the measured water until the dough comes together and the bowl is clean. Cover with a damp tea towel. Set aside while you make the filling.

Now for the filling. Pour the oil into a frying pan over medium heat and cook the onion for 8 minutes until soft. Add the red pepper, tomato, scallions, garlic, thyme, and a pinch of black pepper. Either add the Scotch bonnet, if using, whole, for flavor without too much heat, or finely chop ¼–½ of it and add that for more of a kick. Cook for 8 minutes, adding a splash of water if the pan seems dry. Meanwhile, separately cook the saltfish and remove the skin and bones (see page 18).

Add the saltfish and callaloo to the onion mixture and cook for another 5 minutes, until the sauce has reduced and the greens are soft. Taste for seasoning and add salt if needed. Remove the Scotch bonnet, if whole.

Pour enough oil into a frying pan so it is about 3 in (7.5 cm) deep and place it over medium heat, following all the usual precautions for deep-frying (see page 288). Roll the dough into balls the size of a small mandarin. Test the oil temperature by dropping in a tiny bit of dumpling dough: it should sink at first and then rise and bubble after a few seconds.

Drop the dumplings into the oil and cook for 3–5 minutes until golden, then turn and cook for a further 3 minutes until golden all over, ensuring you keep moving them to get an even color all over. Once ready, transfer the dumplings to a wire rack.

Once cool enough to handle, slice or tear each dumpling open and stuff with the callaloo and saltfish filling. Add a little hot sauce, if you like.

From the Waters

The fruits of the sea have long sustained Jamaicans and the seafood you'll have on the island ranks among the best anywhere in the world. The skills of Jamaican chefs at a seafood cookout are something to behold, as they perfectly execute fried fish, lobster, and shrimp to create a feast that excites while paying homage to cooks who have come before.

These dishes—ackee and saltfish, rundown, pepper shrimp—are rooted in the island's history, revealing how each incoming people's influence has intermingled to create magic.

The recipes also serve as a love letter to dishes I've eaten in Jamaica and can still taste today: janga soup in Castleton, lobster at a Boston jerk pit, and, of course, fried fish. Make it escovitch and enjoy it with bammy, the cassava bread soaking up all those incredible flavors. Eating that, if I close my eyes, I could be back at Treasure Beach, watching the sea lap the near-white sand. Almost.

GINGER BEER SHRIMP

Shrimp have been a mainstay of the Jamaican diet since our knowledge of human history there begins. They were eaten by the indigenous Jamaicans; the Taíno are recorded to have fed Columbus a meal that included them. The sea and rivers remain a source of the crustaceans to this day.

My idea for this dish came from Japanese tempura: the sweet shrimp encased in a light, crispy batter is a dream combination. While tempura calls for soda water, ginger beer is a great alternative. It brings both delicate flavor and sweetness, while the bubbles make the batter as light as air.

SERVES 4 AS AN APPETIZER

16-24 shell-on raw jumbo shrimp
1 garlic clove, crushed
1 in (2.5 cm) piece of ginger, finely grated
vegetable oil, for deep-frying
½ cup (50 g) cornstarch
scant ½ cup (50 g) all-purpose flour
½ cup (120 ml) ice-cold ginger beer (not diet)
sea salt and freshly ground black pepper
lime wedges, to serve

Remove the heads and shells of the shrimp, leaving on the tail sections. (You can also use peeled shrimp, as long as they are raw.) Mix in a bowl with the garlic, ginger, and some ground black pepper and leave for 30 minutes.

Pour oil into a medium-sized pot, following all the usual precautions for deep-frying (see page 288) and heating to 350°F (180°C).

Mix the cornstarch and flour in a bowl and pour in the ginger beer. Stir loosely, as vigorous mixing will get rid of the bubbles you want to keep; don't worry if there are some lumps.

Just before cooking, season the shrimp with a good pinch of salt. Holding a shrimp by the tail, dip into the batter, then drop into the hot oil. Cook until the batter puffs up, about 2 minutes. Repeat to cook all the shrimp, frying them in small batches so as not to overcrowd the pan.

Drain on a wire rack placed over paper towels, not directly on paper towels or the batter will get soggy, and serve with a squeeze of lime.

SHELLFISH WITH LIME & COCONUT

This dish is so evocative for me. The flavors take me to the sun, the sea, and the fresh air, even when I'm stuck in the city with no seaside within a two-hour drive.

The richness of coconut with the added punch from lime and the heat from Scotch bonnet gives so much depth. I like to scoop a bit of broth up with each mouthful and be sure to dunk the shrimp back in once they've been shelled.

You can use any mix of shellfish: cockles and crab claws would work brilliantly. Just make sure to crack the crab claws before cooking, so all that flavor can get in.

SERVES 4-6

2¼ lb (1 kg) live mussels
2¼ lb (1 kg) live clams
6-12 shell-on raw shrimp, depending on size
2 tbsp vegetable oil
2 banana shallots, finely chopped
½ green bell pepper, finely chopped
leaves from 3 thyme sprigs, plus more
    to serve
¼-1 Scotch bonnet, deseeded and
    finely chopped
1 celery stick, finely chopped
scant ½ cup (100 ml) white wine
1¼ cups (300 ml) coconut milk
    (for homemade, see page 271)
2 ears of corn, each cut into 4 rounds
finely grated zest and juice of 3 limes
sea salt and freshly ground black pepper
Hard Dough Bread, to serve (see page 232)

Rinse all the shellfish. Clean the mussels: remove the beards and discard any that are open and won't stay shut after being pressed together.

In a large pot (for which you have a lid), warm the oil over medium heat and fry the shallots, green pepper, thyme, Scotch bonnet to taste, and celery, until softened. Add the wine, coconut milk, corn, and shrimp, stir to combine, then add the mussels and clams. Stir and cover with a lid.

Cook for about 3 minutes until all the mussels and clams have opened (discard any that remain shut) and the shrimp are pink and cooked through.

Finish with the lime juice, stir, then serve sprinkled with the lime zest and a little more thyme. Serve with Hard Dough Bread.

SMOKED MACKEREL RUNDOWN

"Salt-Mackarel are here a great Provision, especially for Negros, who covet them extreamly in Pepper-Pots."
Hans Sloane, *A Voyage to the Islands...* (1707)

Historically, salt mackerel formed a major part of the diet of everyone on the island, both enslaved and free.

The exact origin of rundown, a dish in which the fish is cooked down—hence its name—with coconut and flavorings, is unknown. But in the 18th century it was noted that the enslaved population loved salt mackerel in "pepper pots," where a pot of soup or stew is kept over the fire to cook slowly.

There are records suggesting the indigenous people also cooked in a style described as "pepper pots," that sometimes included extracted cassava juice cooked down until it was no longer poisonous. It's likely rundown was born out of this one-pot tradition that enabled nourishing, hearty meals to be made from whatever ingredients were on hand, with just a little bit of protein.

Here, smoked mackerel adds a lovely dimension to the dish. Because smoked mackerel is ready to eat, you don't need to cook it down for a long time, so it's a relatively quick meal to make.

SERVES 4

1 onion, sliced
vegetable oil
3 garlic cloves, crushed
1 in (2.5 cm) piece of ginger, finely grated
1 red bell pepper, sliced
7 oz (200 g) yellow yam or pumpkin, peeled,
    deseeded if needed, then chopped
2 tomatoes, chopped
½ tsp ground pimento (allspice)
½ tsp ground cumin
leaves from 3 thyme sprigs
1⅔ cups (400 ml) coconut milk
    (for homemade, see page 271)
2 bay leaves
6 smoked mackerel fillets, skin removed

To serve
Lorna's Boiled Dumpling, Boiled Green
    Bananas, Fried Dumpling, or Fried
    Breadfruit (see pages 227, 224, and 219)

Fry the onion in a little oil in a frying pan for 5 minutes until it starts to soften. Add the garlic, ginger, red pepper, yam or pumpkin, tomatoes, spices, and thyme and fry for another 5 minutes before adding the coconut milk and bay leaves. Add a splash of water to loosen, put a lid on, and cook down for 15–20 minutes, until the pumpkin or yam has softened.

Remove the lid, stir in the mackerel, and cook for another 10 minutes until the liquid has thickened.

Serve with Lorna's Boiled Dumpling, Fried Dumpling, Boiled Green Bananas, or Fried Breadfruit.

ACKEE & SALTFISH

When I go to visit my parents and Dad makes this, I'm immediately transported to my childhood. The dish is so evocative for me. Still, to this day, my parents split the tasks: Dad on ackee and saltfish, Mom on plantain and dumpling duty.

Because canned ackee is so expensive, Dad would only use one can and that determined how much could be made. So instead I'd monitor Mom as she mixed the dumpling dough, willing her to make a lot.

This is a dish I always eat with my hands, using torn bits of fried dumpling to scoop up mouthfuls. And I mop up every bit of sauce.

Ackee and saltfish encapsulates the essence of Jamaican food in its conjoining of ingredients from various sources to create something that, to me, is greater than the sum of its parts. Saltfish imported from North America, primarily Canada, was traded with Europe. In the Caribbean, a poorer-quality version called "West India Cure" or "Jamaica Cure"—that would have been rejected by Europeans—was eaten. Salt cod was highly regarded but rarely given to enslaved people, whose rations usually included pickled herring or salted mackerel, which was often putrid, but still featured heavily in their diets. Ackee, in turn, is a fruit that was brought to Jamaica from West Africa on a slave ship in 1778.

The exact moment the two were paired has never been definitively pinpointed, to my knowledge. But perhaps, back when saltfish was not of the highest quality, other ingredients were added to dilute its taste.

SERVES 4

8 oz (225 g) saltfish, rinsed and soaked
   overnight (see page 18)
2 tbsp vegetable oil
½ onion, finely chopped
1 red bell pepper, sliced
2 garlic cloves, crushed
⅓–1 Scotch bonnet, deseeded and finely
   chopped, to taste
2 medium tomatoes, deseeded and chopped
2 scallions, chopped
leaves from 3 thyme sprigs
⅔ cup (150 ml) water
19 oz (540 g) can of ackee, drained

To serve (optional)
Seasoned Callaloo and Fried Dumplings or
   Festival (see pages 111, 224, and 223)

Put the saltfish in a pan of water and bring it to a boil. Simmer until the fish is cooked through and soft; the time this takes will vary depending on the type of fish, so expect anything from 8 up to 20 minutes. Once cooked, drain. When it is cool, break the fish into smaller pieces, checking for bones and removing them as you go and removing the skin as well.

Pour the oil into a frying pan and fry the onion, red pepper, garlic, and Scotch bonnet over medium heat until they soften, without letting them color; 8–10 minutes.

Add the saltfish, cook for 5 minutes, then add the tomatoes, scallions, thyme, and measured water. Cook for a further 5–8 minutes until the tomatoes and scallions soften.

Gently stir in the ackee, being careful not to break the curds up. Warm through for 2–3 minutes.

Serve with Seasoned Callaloo and Fried Dumplings or Festival, or other hard food (see page 283).

A field of sugar cane

Under the English

The Drax Estate

There is a stretch of road in Dorset that fascinated me as a child. Driving along the A31 road with my parents, a low red-brick wall appeared and continued for many miles. Behind it, all I could see were trees. I would keep my eyes glued to mile after mile of the monotonous wall, then, suddenly, there it was: an archway, with a deer standing proudly on top. It was this majestic beast that I would wait for and, once I had seen it, I could sit back, relax, and carry on with the journey.

Back then, I didn't think much about what actually lay behind the wall. But in adulthood I discovered it marked the perimeter of Charborough House, better known to locals as the Drax Estate. At the time of writing, the current owner Richard Drax is the Member of Parliament for South Dorset.

The Drax family is used to power. In 1627, when England claimed the island of Barbados, Richard's ancestors, brothers James and William, were among the English settlers who sailed to the island and bought valuable tracts of land.

In the cargo were ten enslaved Africans, but, at first, the workforce was largely made up of white convicts and indentured Europeans, who would labor for an agreed number of years before earning their freedom, a lump sum of money, and some land. But the enslaved Black workers had no such benefits; their enslavement was forever.

Quickly, landowners such as James Drax began to favor Black labor; even though the initial outlay might be higher, owners' possession was absolute. It was seen as a better investment. Within thirty years, more than eighty percent of the land on Barbados was being used for sugar plantations and Black Africans outnumbered white Europeans twice over. English plantation owners had established the island as a slave society, creating a blueprint that would be repeated throughout the Caribbean.

Of course, at that time, slavery was nothing new, and the transportation of captive Africans by Europeans had been happening for centuries. But under the English it was transformed into a wholesale business; barbarity on an industrial scale previously impossible to imagine.

Between the 16th and 19th centuries, about twelve-and-a-half *million* people from West and Central Africa were kidnapped and sold as human chattels by European nations in the transatlantic trade. The "triangular route" saw goods exported from Europe to Africa, in exchange for African men and women, gold, ivory, and spices, who were taken to the Americas. Before the abolition of the slave trade, British slave traders were responsible for the forced transportation of more than three million West Africans.

Discovering this physical connection to slavery so close to my childhood home was a shock. It felt personal. But I shouldn't have been surprised. The day-to-day violence of industrial slavery may have played out thousands of miles away from British soil, but evidence of it is all around. It is in street names, in the statues of slavers that we walk past every day in cities, villages, and parks up and down Britain, and in the very foundations of some of our most prized buildings. In a sense, slavery built Britain.

But we were not taught about that at school. It didn't feature on our national curriculum and only relatively recently has this appalling part of Britain's history started to be addressed. It is almost as though the story is so shameful that Britain has tried to erase it.

But it is important. Its repercussions are still felt today.

In Europe, the transatlantic slave trade fostered a delusion of racial superiority that persists. In Africa, it created a deep sense of unease and fear, exacerbated tribal conflict, and led to global economic disadvantage through depopulation. And in Jamaica, it led to a societal inequality that exists to this day, as it does in many former British colonies.

The mass relocation of millions of people from different African nations and multifarious tribes had a huge impact on Jamaica. The enslaved Africans brought what remnants of their home lifestyle they could salvage with them to the island, in the teeth of the near-impossible conditions of the journey. They brought their expertise in agriculture and animal husbandry, their stories and songs, as well as food, crops, cooking methods, and flavors.

The Sugar Revolution

As early English plantation owners had learned, the weather throughout the Caribbean made it the perfect region for very large agricultural yields. Thanks to rapidly rising demand in Europe, cotton, tobacco, rice, and sugar were now important cash crops. Sugar, the most popular of all, was dangerous to produce and hugely intensive, requiring a large labor force to plant, tend, and harvest the cane, then gruelling work in boiling houses to process it into sugar. It was then transported to Europe in barrels.

Previously, sugar's astronomical price tag had made it the preserve only of the very wealthy, but its growing availability had forced prices down and ordinary Europeans were getting a taste for it. By the latter half of the 17th century, business on the sugar plantations of Barbados was booming; the island was now the leading exporter of sugar, something of a feat considering its modest size.

The success of the plantations on Barbados had proved the potential of a business model built on English money, New World territory, and forced African labor. The English had created what they deemed to be a successful slave society, and they were proud of it. Jamaica came next.

At dawn on 21 May 1655, an English expedition force entered Caguaya Bay and, with Jamaica of waning interest to its Spanish colonizers, captured the island against relatively little resistance. Their enslaved Africans were either set free or escaped and took refuge in the mountains where they fought off attempts at recapture and eventually built free agricultural communities. Their leaders, including Nanny and Cudjoe, are still revered today.

Elsewhere, the island was soon swallowed up with plantations, with names such as Mesopotamia, Cinnamon Hill, and Roehampton. And as Europe's insatiable desire for sugar grew, so did the forced transportations of African men, women, and children to produce it.

The business of international slavery was complex, requiring the cooperation of people across all the continents in which it operated. English ships began their journey in the major shipping ports, the three most popular being Bristol, Liverpool, and London. All three cities prospered greatly from the trade, its beneficiaries amassing huge generational wealth.

The ships touted for crew and stocked up on tradeable goods and supplies before heading to the West Coast of Africa. Here, the trade in humans occurred along a 3,000-mile stretch that covered modern-day Senegal, Gambia, and Guinea Bissau, down to the so-called Gold Coast, then into Gabon, Congo, and Angola; it came to be known as the "Slave Coast." Some of those sold into slavery were prisoners of war from conflicts between rival kingdoms, traded with the Europeans in return for firearms. Other rulers resisted the trade, so, as the demand for slave labor increased, Europeans relied increasingly on a vast network of middlemen to capture people and bring them to the coast.

Born in what is now southern Nigeria around 1745, Olaudah Equiano was sold into slavery as a child. He eventually bought his freedom aged twenty and became an important voice in the abolitionist movement. In his *An Interesting Narrative of the Life of Olaudah Equiano*, he gave valuable and rare insight into the plight of the enslaved. He wrote that the fear of kidnap was an everyday reality during his childhood. Aged eleven, those fears were realized "when an end was put to my happiness."

> "Generally, when the grown people in the neighborhood were gone far in the fields to labor, the children assembled together in some of the neighbors' premises to play; and commonly some of us used to get up

a tree to look out for any assailant, or kidnapper, that might come upon us; for they sometimes took those opportunities of our parents' absence to attack and carry off as many as they could seize.

"One day, when all our people were gone out to their works as usual, and only I and my dear sister were left to mind the house, two men and a woman got over our walls and seized us both, and without giving us time to cry out, or make resistance, they stopped our mouths and ran off with us into the nearest wood. Here they tied our hands, and continued to carry us as far as they could, until night came on, when we reached a small house… and spent the night."

The captives were chained and forced on a long march—Equiano recalled traveling for six to seven months—and some died along the way. Once they reached the coastline, the captives were held in forts until their ships were ready. The men were stripped naked, branded with a hot iron, and loaded below deck where they were each bolted to another man with leg irons to prevent escape. The space was so cramped that the men were forced to lie in rows, usually on their sides. The ships remained docked until they were at full capacity, so often captives would spend weeks in the belly of a ship, held in chains, before the convoy even set sail.

Women and children were kept on deck. Rape by their captors was common and physical violence frequent: overseers would use the whip willingly. Suicide attempts were thwarted at any cost and punished by flogging. Executions were carried out as a last resort, usually for uprisings against the crew.

Many of the enslaved had never even seen the sea before and seasickness was rife; sanitation was non-existent and so the crushed space below deck flowed with excrement and vomit. Unsurprisingly, disease and illness prevailed, including smallpox and dysentery. The many who died during what became known as the Middle Passage were simply thrown overboard.

Equiano described his terror at first seeing Europeans on the ships. When he saw a "large furnace of copper boiling" he believed he was going to be "eaten by those white men with horrible looks, red faces and long hair."

Below deck he met with an unbearable stench, his fellow captives wearing "countenances expressing dejection and sorrow."

The stream in Richmond where my father grew up, and where he caught crayfish

"The closeness of the place, and the heat of the climate, added to the number in the ship, which was so crowded that each had scarcely room to turn himself, almost suffocated us. This produced copious perspirations so that the air soon become unfit for respiration from a variety of loathsome smells, and brought on a sickness among the slaves, of which many died, thus falling victim to the improvident avarice of their purchasers. This wretched situation was again aggravated by the galling of the chains, and the filth of the necessary tubs, the shrieks of the women, and the groans of the dying, rendered the whole scene a horror almost inconceivable."

The voyage to the Americas, or the Caribbean colonies, lasted six to eight weeks. Although the human cargo was insured, if anyone died onboard a claim could not be brought for the money. However, a proportion of deaths were expected and seen merely as collateral damage. Twice a day the men were brought up to the deck for food, often rice or peas; they were watched to ensure everyone ate, and any who refused were force-fed and flogged. An estimated 1.8 million captured Africans died at sea. Many more were slaughtered in Africa itself during the violence of capture, or on their long journeys to the ships.

The majority of the enslaved Africans were transported to the Caribbean. And Jamaica took among the most of any island, close to 700,000 men, women, and children. When the ships docked, the traders unloaded their human cargo and washed and oiled their skin; with their appearance improved, the enslaved Africans could attract a better price. Payment was often made with a bill of exchange, a system introduced by the Royal African Company, who for a while held the monopoly of the transatlantic slave trade. The bills would be passed between planters, to ships' captains, then to slave merchants back in Britain. Once sold, families were separated: children torn from parents, husbands from their wives, and brothers and sisters divided, never to see each other again.

Life in Jamaica

When they walked off the slave ships in Jamaica, enslaved people had to adapt to a completely new way of life. Plantation governors set about "seasoning" the arrivals, drilling them in the rules that bound them and the labor expected. This took up to three years; many did not survive it. Malnourishment, disease, or injury were common causes of death; others sought solace in suicide.

> "The Negroes from some Countries think they return to their own Country when they die in Jamaica, and therefore regard death but little, imagining they shall change their condition, by that means from servile to free, and so for this reason often cut their own Throats."

Under their new masters, the enslaved had little independence and the threat of brutality overshadowed their every waking moment. Physical violence was an everyday occurrence, both punitive and pre-emptive to subdue resistance. Equiano witnessed "many cruel punishments." On one occasion a man was kept hanging by his wrists with weights attached to his ankles, "in which posture he was flogged most unmercifully."

Hans Sloane, an English-Irish botanist and physician to the island's governor, was stationed in Jamaica during the two-year period 1687–89. He witnessed the masters rubbing salt and pepper into the wounds of flogging victims "to make them smart." "At other times their Masters will drop melted Wax on their skins, and use several very exquisite Torments," he wrote in *A Voyage to the Islands Madera, Barbados, Nieves, S. Christophers and Jamaica* (1707 and 1725).

The European masters had no qualms about abusing enslaved women; rape was rife. Whether through consensual relationships between the enslaved or through rape, any child born to an enslaved woman was born into slavery. This was sometimes seen as a legitimate way to bolster the worker population and thus to become less reliant on importation over time. As soon as the children were able to walk and follow instruction, they could be given tasks.

Most of the enslaved worked on sugar plantations; others tended livestock, some worked in domestic settings. In the cane fields, the enslaved were divided into gangs with different responsibilities depending on age and fitness. Working hours were sunrise to sunset. During peak harvest times, people were forced to work the "long spell" on the field all day cutting cane, then throughout the night in the factory, then returning to the field for another full day's labor before getting a break. The longer days proved the most dangerous, especially in the boiling house, where workers operated heavy machinery to crush sugar cane to extract the juice; those too exhausted to concentrate risked mutilation or sustaining devastating injuries. Mortality, unsurprisingly, was high.

The only respite came on Sundays and public holidays, and sometimes Saturday afternoons, which were granted as leave. The enslaved came from a multitude of African tribes—Akan, Yoruba, and Igbo—and as much as possible, they maintained their traditions. Sundays in Jamaica were often market days, where the enslaved would take surplus produce to sell. This proved a vital, lasting part of the food culture that grew out of the provision ground system.

The enslaved received meager rations of beef, pork, and salted fish, as well as cassava bread, yams, and potatoes. To supplement these often poor-quality offerings, the workers were permitted to grow what they could for themselves on "provision grounds." But as sugar plantations spread over more and more of the prime land, the workers were forced into isolated spots with difficult terrain. Sometimes they were allowed to rear livestock, usually chickens and occasionally pigs, but for the most part their rations were insufficient.

Starchy tubers such as yam, dasheen, cassava, and sweet potato, therefore, were the most popular crops; they fare well in poor soil, require relatively little cultivation, are filling and are high in energy. Today they are still boiled and served alongside a main meal.

Rebellion & Emancipation

Despite the might of the imperialist powers, the transatlantic slave trade met with resistance at every stage. From the boat crews who would try to release people from slave ships as they left ports along the African coast, to the rebellions that took place on plantations, and even though insurrection meant certain death on capture, the African people continued to fight for freedom.

Throughout the centuries, barely a decade passed without an uprising, some involving thousands of people. The Maroons began their rebellion against the English as soon as they arrived in Jamaica and were a constant threat to British rule. In Tacky's Revolt, April 1760, Tacky—thought to have been a chief from Guinea—led one hundred of his fellow slaves to take over a plantation in the northern parish of St. Mary. After overpowering British forces and killing their captors, Tacky and his men enjoyed brief freedom, before their recapture and execution.

The Haitian Revolution, under Toussaint Louverture, between 1791 and 1804, saw the enslavers expelled and the island became the first to be ruled by formerly enslaved people since the Europeans' arrival. The successful revolt buoyed enslaved communities throughout the islands, prompting more uprisings. Although no single uprising in Jamaica had such profound success, the authorities were increasingly under pressure. The unrest belied the widely held belief in pro-slavery circles that many of the enslaved were happy to be under the rule of their masters.

As the 18th-century trade continued, prominent European figures rose in support of abolition of the transatlantic trade. Accounts from former enslaved people, such as Olaudah Equiano, were invaluable. After buying his freedom and settling in London, the publication of *An Interesting Narrative* in 1789 sent shockwaves throughout the country. It was one of the rare instances that a voice had been given to the millions of people forced into violent servitude.

The Anglican Thomas Clarkson, and Alexander Falconbridge, a former slave ship's surgeon, spent their lives leading the campaign for an end to slavery.

Josiah Wedgewood boosted support for the abolition movement by designing a seal featuring a chained man, bearing the inscription *"Am I Not a Man and a Brother?,"* while the publication of an illustration of the Brooks slave ship (see page 292) offered the public a stark vision of the horrors of the enforced slave shipments across the Atlantic. Support for the abolition movement grew steadily throughout the end of the 18th century until, in 1807, the Slave Trade Abolition Bill received Royal Assent. But it did not go far enough, and in 1833 the Abolition of Slavery Act—brought into effect in 1834—marked the beginning of the end for slavery in British territories.

A Free Nation?

But the transition from a slave society to a free one did not happen overnight. Those "freed" from slavery were required to continue to work for their former owners as apprentices until 1838. It was a gradual emancipation put in place ostensibly to ease the enslaved population's transition to freedom, but was in fact more to protect the business interests of their British enslavers.

Children under the age of six were immediately freed, field hands were apprenticed for six years, while household laborers were to work for four. The apprentices worked for forty-five hours per week for free, though they were compensated for any additional work. An apprentice could buy his or her freedom if they had saved enough to pay the remaining years of their service. The deal saw workers agree to a fixed term of employment plus the offer of transport back to their country of origin, though many chose to remain.

To make up the labor shortfall, the British now looked to their Indian colony for indentured servants (who were contracted to work for a certain number of years to pay off their servitude). Chinese indentured servants also came to the island, though in smaller numbers. Today Indo-Jamaicans and Chinese-Jamaicans make up the biggest immigrant communities in Jamaica.

No Black people from the lands in Africa, where millions of people were captured, nor the vast majority of Jamaicans who are descended from the enslaved, have ever received a penny in reparations or compensation for what the Europeans did to them and their ancestors.

Instead, under the Slave Compensation Act of 1837, the slave owners received compensation for their losses. One John Drax (a descendent of James Drax) was awarded £4,293 12s 6d (worth almost $400,000 today) for the one hundred and eighty-nine enslaved people who were held at Drax Hall in Barbados.

Treasure Beach, St. Elizabeth

FRIED FISH

This is a favored preparation of delicately spiced fish in Jamaica. It's a really delicious, pleasing food and a must-have at gatherings. Though as a child I wasn't a fan, now I can't get enough, especially if the fish is "escovitched."

Escovitch has its roots in Spain's Jewish settlers (the word comes from the Spanish *escabeche*), who moved to Jamaica as early as the 16th century to escape persecution during the Spanish Inquisition. According to the Jewish Museum, by 1720 about 18 percent of the Jamaican population was Jewish.

The vinegary sauce here has to be balanced correctly, otherwise it can be overpowering, so be careful with how much you use.

SERVES 4

For the fried fish
1 tsp onion powder
1 tsp garlic powder
1 tsp ground pimento (allspice)
1 tsp freshly ground black pepper
1 tsp sea salt
4 whole snapper, or sea bass, or sea bream,
    gutted and cleaned
4 tbsp all-purpose flour
vegetable oil, for deep-frying
Bammy, to serve (see page 197)

For the escovitch
1 large carrot, cut into matchsticks
1 large white onion, cut into matchsticks
    lengthways
½ red bell pepper, cut into matchsticks
    lengthways
⅓ cup (80 ml) water
2 tbsp apple cider vinegar or
    white wine vinegar
1 tbsp sugar
1 tsp sea salt

Mix the spices together with the salt. Rinse the fish and score it 3 times on each side. Season the inside of the fish with the spice mixture and, if there's any left, season the outside too.

Put the flour in a dish, season it with salt and pepper, and dip the fish in the seasoned flour, working quickly so the fish doesn't dry out as the flour needs moisture to adhere.

Put enough oil in a deep, wide pan so it is 2 in (5 cm) deep, following all the usual precautions for deep-frying (see page 288). Heat it to 350°F (180°C) and fry the fish for 3 minutes on each side.

Now for the escovitch. Put the vegetables in a sauté pan with the measured water. Cook for 2 minutes, then add the vinegar, sugar, and salt. Stir to combine, then cook for a further 5 minutes until the liquid has reduced by half and the vegetables are starting to soften.

Pour the escovitch over the fish and serve with Bammy.

SALTFISH, BUTTER BEAN & RED PEPPER STEW

We were driving back to Kingston when we passed a row of huts at Hope Village in Mandeville, each one serving something slightly different. I'd overshot, so I had to do a U-turn, but it was totally worth it. There was a woman called Shelley whose roasted yam and breadfruit was something else. She served it with a saltfish and red pepper stew, which seemed almost secondary to the roasted hard food, but it really stuck in my memory. I made it a few times, adding butter beans to add another texture into the dish, and I love it. Once the saltfish is soaked it is a really quick, satisfying dish to make.

SERVES 4

14 oz (400 g) saltfish, rinsed and soaked
   (see page 18)
1 large onion, sliced
vegetable oil
3 garlic cloves, crushed
1 red bell pepper, sliced
leaves from 3 thyme sprigs
1 tsp ground pimento (allspice)
1 tsp freshly ground black pepper
14 oz (400 g) can of butter beans, drained
1¼ cups (300 ml) vegetable stock
   (for homemade, see page 127)
sea salt

To serve
Festival, Roasted Breadfruit, or plain rice
   and plantain (see pages 223, 219,
   and 214-215)

Boil the saltfish until it is soft and cooked through. Once it's cool enough to handle, break it up, checking for bones and removing them along with the skin as you go.

In a frying pan, fry the onion in a splash of oil until softened. Add the garlic and red pepper and cook for a further 8 minutes. Add the thyme, pimento, and black pepper and cook, stirring, until you can smell all the aromatics.

Add the fish and drained beans, pour in the stock, and simmer for 10 minutes until the sauce thickens slightly. Taste for seasoning and add salt if needed, though it may be salty enough already because of the fish.

Serve with Festival, Roasted Breadfruit, or plain rice and plantain.

GRILLED LOBSTER WITH SCALLION & PEPPER BUTTER

Lobster is abundant in the Caribbean waters and in Jamaica it is often served grilled, which I think brings out the best of its flavor: there is some interaction between the meat and the charring shells that makes it really special.

This recipe is based on a lobster dish I ate at I & R Boston Jerk Centre at Boston Beach in Portland. There, the lobsters were cooked in foil with butter, pepper, and scallions, plus a few other bits. I think the foil was for convenience, so the lobsters could be thrown onto the fire to order. I don't bother with foil and cook them directly on the coals. In this recipe I used a European lobster. The spiny lobsters of the Caribbean—also known as rock lobsters—as well as North American varieties will also work well in this recipe.

SERVES 4

½ cup (110 g) salted butter, at room temperature

½–1 Scotch bonnet, finely chopped, deseeded or not depending on heat tolerance

2 scallions, finely chopped

1 tsp freshly ground black pepper

1 garlic clove, crushed

½ tsp ground pimento (allspice)

1 tsp sea salt

2 limes, zested and cut into wedges

4 lobsters (ideally live for maximum freshness, but use cooked if that's all you can get)

a little flavorless oil

To serve (optional)
Cassava Fries and Mango & Grapefuit Salad, (see pages 220 and 24)

First, prepare the butter. In a bowl, mix together the butter with the Scotch bonnet, scallions, black pepper, garlic, pimento, salt, and lime zest. Set aside.

Get a barbecue ready for indirect cooking, with the coals piled on one side. Make sure the cooking grate has been brushed down and is clean, to prevent the lobsters from sticking.

If using live lobsters, take each one and lay it flat on a chopping board. To dispatch a lobster quickly and humanely, point your knife at the base of the head so the blade is over the head. Insert the knife and quickly bring it down so you cut the head in half, rendering it dead instantly. Turn the knife around and repeat the same movement to cut the body in half.

Open the lobster up and remove the dark green part from the head with a spoon. Finally, crack the shell of the largest claw with the back of the knife. Repeat with the 3 remaining lobsters. Clean the board between each lobster and only kill them when you're ready to cook them, as the meat spoils quickly.

Rub a thin layer of oil on the cut surface of the lobsters and, once the coals are ready—ashy-looking, with no flame—place the lobsters cut sides down on the grate. Leave for a couple of minutes, to get a bit of color on them, then turn the lobsters over so the cut sides are facing up, and move them away from the direct heat.

Place slices of the flavored butter across the flesh sides of the lobsters so they are fully covered. Close the lid of the barbecue and leave for 3–4 minutes until the lobster meat is cooked through.

Serve with the lime wedges and with Cassava Fries and Mango & Grapefruit Salad, if you like.

GRILLED SHRIMP WITH LIME, CHILE & BROWN BUTTER

This dish is a lesson in simplicity. The flavors are really subtle, just enlivened by the brown butter, which in itself is a lovely pairing with any shellfish.

This isn't a dish from Jamaica, but it's certainly heavily inspired by the island's cooking.

SERVES 4 AS AN APPETIZER

20 shell-on raw jumbo shrimp
11 tbsp (150 g) unsalted butter
a little vegetable oil
1 lime, zested and halved
¼–½ Scotch bonnet (depending on heat tolerance), finely chopped
1 scallion, green part only, finely sliced
sea salt

Using scissors, cut through the shell of the shrimp down the back, starting at the end next to the head and stopping before you get to the final segment attached to the tail. Use a toothpick to pull the black vein away from the body, pulling it gently towards the tail. Discard.

Heat the butter in a saucepan over medium heat for 5 minutes, until it starts to foam. Turn off.

Put a splash of oil in a frying pan over medium-high heat and add the shrimp. Turn frequently, cooking for about 7 minutes in total, until the shrimp are pink and starting to char and there is no grey visible.

Transfer the shrimp to 4 plates and sprinkle with the lime zest, Scotch bonnet, and scallion. Squeeze the juice of half the zested lime over the shrimp on each plate and finish with a good pinch of salt.

Heat the butter up again and wait for the foam to die down and for it to start to smell nutty. Pour over each of the shrimp. Serve with the remaining half lime, cut into 4 wedges.

Eat immediately, and make sure that once you take the shell off the shrimp, you rub each in the butter and grab up the chile and scallion before popping it into your mouth.

CASTLETON JANGA SOUP

We were driving to Portland from Kingston, with my friend Jaxx Nelson and photographer Aaron Dabee, when Jaxx got a hunch about a good soup spot. We reached a little place in Castleton with food vendors, jerk pans, and patties, and right out front were big pots of soup being stirred on wheel rim cooking grates packed with glowing coals.

Jaxx recalled having a good janga soup there a few years back. Thankfully, the same seller was there and we each ordered a cup. A prized janga—crayfish—sat on top of each cup, its claw hanging over the edge, while lurking in the steaming orange depths were loads of hard food and shrimp. It was so good that I burnt my bottom lip, too impatient to let it cool down properly.

This soup takes me back to that special time. It is also dear to me because I associate janga with my dad, who caught them in the stream at the bottom of his family's land as a boy. I've been to the same stream with Dad's cousin Patsy, who is also a pro at catching them. Me, not so much; my reflexes are too slow, though I did get one.

The dish is really peppery, but the heat builds slowly rather than knocking your socks off with the first mouthful.

SERVES 6

For the stock
1 lb (500 g) shell-on raw shrimp, peeled, shells and heads reserved
vegetable oil
1 garlic clove, crushed
1 bay leaf
sea salt and freshly ground black pepper

For the soup
10½ oz (300 g) pumpkin, peeled, deseeded, and cut into ½ in (1 cm) cubes
4 scallions, finely chopped
1 garlic clove, crushed
1 in (2.5 cm) piece of ginger, finely grated
1 tsp mixed dried herbs
½ tsp ground turmeric
1 tsp all-purpose seasoning
1 tsp freshly ground black pepper
1 Scotch bonnet
8½ cups (2 liters) vegetable stock
1 tsp ground pimento (allspice)
1 white or sweet potato, cut into cubes
10½ oz (300 g) yam, cut into ½ in (1 cm) cubes
2 tbsp all-purpose flour
1 lb (450 g) shell-on crayfish or jumbo shrimp

For the stock, fry the shrimp shells and heads in a pot in some oil with the garlic, bay leaf, pepper, and a pinch of salt for 5 minutes. Add 4¼ cups (1 liter) of water, bring to a boil, and simmer until the liquid has reduced by half. Strain into a bowl and discard the shells and bay leaf, then pour into a large pot.

Add the pumpkin to the liquid. Cook until soft, then blend until smooth.

In a large pot, fry the scallions, garlic, and ginger in a little more oil for 8 minutes. Add the dried herbs, turmeric, all-purpose seasoning, black pepper, and Scotch bonnet—either whole for flavor or ¼–½ finely chopped for heat, to taste—to the scallions with a splash of water and cook for 5 minutes, or until all the water has evaporated.

Pour in the vegetable stock and pumpkin mixture, pimento, potato, and yam, then bring to a boil and simmer for 30 minutes. Put the flour in a small bowl, add a couple of tablespoons of liquid from the soup, and mix until there are no lumps. Mix this back into the soup. Stir and cook for another 20 minutes.

Add the janga (crayfish) or jumbo shrimp, as well as the shrimp you used to make the stock, and cook until they are pink. Taste for seasoning and add as much salt as you think you need, up to 1 teaspoon. Remove the whole Scotch bonnet, if using, then serve.

Janga soup seller in Castleton

PEPPER SHRIMP

A proper slap-you-upside-the-head dish. Pepper shrimp are sold in bags in Jamaica and even though the heat will get your top lip sweaty in no time, you'll be coming back for more.

The area best known for them is Middle Quarters in St. Elizabeth, where vendors line up with their red shrimp caught in the nearby Black River, though often supplemented from elsewhere too.

SERVES 4 AS AN APPETIZER OR SNACK

1 lb 5 oz (600 g) shell-on raw crayfish or
    jumbo shrimp
1–2 Scotch bonnets, deseeded or not
    depending on heat tolerance,
    finely chopped
3 garlic cloves, crushed
½ onion, finely chopped
½ tsp ground pimento (allspice)
½ tsp freshly ground black pepper
2 tsp onion powder
2 tsp garlic powder
1 tsp dried thyme
1 tsp sea salt
1 tbsp vegetable oil, plus more for cooking
1 tsp annatto seeds or annatto paste

Remove the antennae and legs from the shrimp and devein (see page 83). Mix with all the other ingredients apart from the annatto and leave for 30 minutes.

Heat 3 tablespoons of oil in a wide frying pan over medium heat and add the annatto seeds or paste, stirring occasionally. Cook for 5 minutes until the oil is red and then remove the seeds, if using.

Separate the shrimp from their marinade and cook the marinade in the same oil until the onion softens, 5–7 minutes. Add the shrimp, stir to fully coat, then add just a splash of water to cook through, not to make a sauce. Put the lid on, swirl the pan around, and leave for 2 minutes to steam.

Remove the shrimp from the mixture and serve.

THYME STUFFED SNAPPER

The simplicity of the aromatics works really well in this dish. Steaming sends the scent of thyme throughout the fish, leaving it delicately flavored. It's a favorite of my daughter, who adores fish and likes an unfussy approach. Try to get as fresh a fish as possible.

SERVES 2–4

2 tbsp apple cider vinegar

2 tbsp water

1 tsp sugar

½ red onion, finely sliced

1 red bell pepper, finely sliced

4 tomatoes, sliced

olive or canola oil

2 scallions, green and white parts
   separated, finely sliced lengthways

1 large bunch of thyme

2 in (5 cm) piece of ginger, finely sliced
   into matchsticks

2–4 whole snapper (sea bream is a
   good alternative), gutted and cleaned

sea salt and freshly ground black pepper

In a saucepan, heat the vinegar with the measured water and add the sugar and a pinch of salt. Pour this over the red onion and red pepper in a bowl, scrunch, and leave to cool.

Divide the tomatoes among individual serving plates, or place them on a platter, top with the pickled red onion and red pepper, and drizzle with oil. Set aside.

Divide the scallions, thyme sprigs, and ginger between the fish and stuff inside the cavities. Add pepper and season with salt.

Prepare a steamer with water and bring to a boil. Lay the fish on top, close the lid, and steam for 10 minutes. Carefully peel a bit of flesh away from the bone to check it's cooked through.

Carefully lift the fish and place on to the pile of tomatoes, pepper, and onion. Serve.

Provision Grounds

Jamaica has led the way in plant-based food for decades. It's little wonder, given the sheer variety of fruit and vegetables found on the island, as well as the prohibitive cost of meat that has historically made it an addition to dishes rather than the central player.

But the Rastafari movement birthed a way of eating that put unadulterated nourishment from the ground front and center. Ital food shops are found everywhere on the island and, although often small, the quality of the food they serve up will take your breath away.

Not everything in this chapter is strictly Ital, which at its purest shuns salt and anything remotely processed. But the food here is all vegan, wholesome, and—most importantly—tasty.

From top left: yam; medium-ripe plantain; ripe plantain; green plantain; avocado ("pear" in Jamaica); breadfruit sliced and whole; green bananas; avocado; callaloo; chocho (chayote); yellow yam

JERK BUTTERNUT SQUASH

Butternut squash is great jerked. The natural sweetness comes into its own through the barbecue's heat, while the pepperiness of the marinade gives a lovely contrast.

SERVES 4-6

1 butternut squash, quartered lengthways
  and deseeded
1 in (2.5 cm) piece of ginger, roughly chopped
1 scallion, roughly chopped
¼ small onion, roughly chopped
1 tsp dried pimento (allspice) berries
¼ tsp ground cinnamon
¼ tsp ground nutmeg
1 tsp sea salt
1 tsp sugar
2 garlic cloves
3 thyme sprigs, roughly stripped
1 tbsp white wine vinegar, or cider vinegar
1 tsp freshly ground black pepper
½ Scotch bonnet

For the vegan jerk gravy
½ onion, roughly chopped
2 scallions, roughly chopped
2 in (5 cm) piece of ginger, chopped
2 garlic cloves
1 tsp ground pimento (allspice)
1 tsp freshly ground black pepper
1 tsp brown sugar
leaves from 2 thyme stalks
¼ Scotch bonnet (optional)
2 tbsp vegetable oil
2 cups (500 ml) vegetable stock (see page 127)
4 tbsp ketchup
1 tsp soy sauce
1 tbsp cornstarch

To serve
Roasted Breadfruit or Rice & Peas
  (see pages 219 and 231)

To barbecue (optional)
a lot of bay branches and leaves
applewood chips, soaked for 30 minutes
cupful of dried pimento (allspice) berries,
  soaked for at least 30 minutes

Take each quarter of squash and slice from the core at 1 in (2.5 cm) intervals, being careful not to cut through the whole vegetable. Blend all the remaining ingredients together in a food processor and pour over the squash, pushing the marinade into the slits.

If using a lidded barbecue, light it for indirect cooking with coals on one side. Once ready and the temperature is 350–400°F (180–200°C), lay the bay leaves on the grill away from the coals. Sprinkle some applewood chips over the bay and the rest over the coals. Put the squash on top of the bay and applewood chips. Sprinkle the soaked pimento on the grill above the coals; don't worry if some fall through. Close the lid, making sure the top vents are open, and smoke for 20 minutes. Open the lid, put the squash on a heatproof tray and sprinkle a couple of tablespoons of water on the tray. Cover tightly with foil and cook on the grill for 45–60 minutes until tender. Remove the foil and cook for a final 10 minutes.

If cooking in an oven, preheat to 350°F (180°C), put the squash on a baking sheet, and bake for 1 hour.

Meanwhile, make the gravy. In a food processor, whizz the onion, scallions, ginger, garlic, pimento, black pepper, sugar, thyme, and Scotch bonnet (if using) so it makes a paste. Heat the oil in a saucepan and fry the paste for 4 minutes over medium heat, stirring regularly. Add the stock, ketchup, and soy sauce and cook for 15 minutes, being sure to scrape the bottom of the pan regularly.

Mix the cornstarch with a splash of water, stirring to form a loose paste. Stir into the gravy and cook until it starts to thicken. Taste for seasoning and add salt if needed.

Serve the squash with the gravy and with Roasted Breadfruit or Rice & Peas.

VIV'S BAKED EGGPLANT IN COCONUT MILK

This is my dad's recipe and perhaps that's why I find it so comforting. It's easy to make and quite similar to my Smoky Eggplant Rundown (see page 112), but different enough to mean they both get made in our home.
I like it served with plain steamed rice, the delicately flavored sauce poured over the top. It's a proper treat.

SERVES 4

4 eggplants
2 medium onions, sliced
3 garlic cloves, sliced
1 Scotch bonnet, deseeded and
    finely chopped
leaves from 1 thyme sprig
14 oz (400 ml) can of coconut milk
    (for homemade, see page 127)
sea salt and freshly ground black pepper

To serve
Boiled Green Bananas (see page 227)
    and rice

Preheat the oven to 350°F (180°C).

Slice the eggplants lengthways into ¼ in (5 mm)-thick slices. Layer half the slices in an ovenproof dish, followed by half the onions. Then top with the garlic, Scotch bonnet, thyme, salt, and pepper. Repeat with the remaining eggplants and onion. Pour the coconut milk over them and cover the dish with foil.

Bake for 40 minutes, then remove the foil and bake for another 15 minutes. Remove from the oven and serve with Boiled Green Bananas and rice.

COCONUT & BLACK-EYED PEA SOUP

I was really fascinated by black-eyed peas as a kid. I remember my dad looking for them in shops and the name really tickled me.

Black-eyed peas, also known as cow peas, were cultivated in West Africa and were vital sustenance on slave ships across the Middle Passage (see page 67), making up a large part of the enslaved people's diet. Introduced to Jamaica in the 17th century (around 1675), they then spread through the West Indies and on to mainland America.

SERVES 4–6

1 onion, chopped
3 garlic cloves, crushed
1 in (2.5 cm) piece of ginger, crushed
1 tbsp vegetable oil
2 carrots, finely chopped
7 oz (200 g) yam, peeled and cubed
7 oz (200 g) pumpkin, peeled, deseeded,
   and cubed
3 thyme sprigs
1 tsp dried mixed herbs
   (Badia is a great brand)
½ tsp ground turmeric
1 Scotch bonnet
1 tsp ground pimento (allspice)
2 tsp all-purpose seasoning
5 cups (1.2 liters) vegetable stock
   (for homemade, see page 127)
14 oz (400 ml) can of coconut milk
   (for homemade, see page 271)
3½ oz (100 g) dried black-eyed peas,
   soaked overnight
2 tbsp all-purpose flour
sea salt and freshly ground black pepper
Spinners, to serve (optional, see page 228)

In a large saucepan, fry off the onion, garlic, and ginger in the oil for 5 minutes until soft and fragrant. Add the carrots, yam, pumpkin, thyme, dried herbs, turmeric, Scotch bonnet (either whole for flavor or ¼–½ finely chopped for heat, to taste), pimento, all-purpose seasoning, salt, and pepper and cook for 5 minutes.

Pour in the stock and coconut milk and cook for 15 minutes, then add the drained black-eyed peas and cook for another 15 minutes, until the vegetables are tender.

Put the flour in a cup, add a couple of spoons of the soup, and stir to make a paste. Keep adding more soup until the flour solution is liquid enough to mix in, then add it to the soup. Cook for 10 minutes, then fish out the thyme sprigs, if you want, as well as the whole Scotch bonnet, if using.

If you want Spinners in the soup, add them to cook as on page 228, then serve.

PEANUT & SWEET POTATO STEW

This dish is unashamedly West African, where peanut stews are common. Yet I've included it here because the movement of peanuts around the world tells of the trading routes that saw food, goods, and people cross the Atlantic through the Columbian Exchange and beyond. The Spanish are said to have taken them back to Spain following their exploration of the so-called New World, where they were planted. From there they were taken to Africa, probably through trade, before being returned to the Americas during the transatlantic slave trade.

Today, peanuts grow throughout Jamaica, especially in St. Elizabeth. So while this isn't a Jamaican dish, it's one that draws on the West African influence that has inspired island food.

SERVES 4-6

1 onion, chopped
vegetable oil
2 garlic cloves, crushed
1 in (2.5 cm) piece of ginger, finely grated
2 tsp ground turmeric
1 tbsp ground cumin
1 tbsp ground coriander
1 tsp ground fenugreek seeds
2 sweet potatoes, peeled and chopped
   into 1 in (2.5 cm) cubes
1⅔ cups (400 ml) vegetable stock
   (for homemade, see page 127)
14 oz (400 g) can of red kidney beans,
   drained
2 tbsp peanut butter
2 mature bunches of spinach, washed and
   roughly chopped, coarse stalks removed
sea salt
boiled rice, to serve

In a Dutch pot or other large, heavy pot, fry the onion in a little oil. After 8 minutes, add the garlic and ginger and cook for another couple of minutes before adding the spices, mixed with a little water to prevent them burning. Stir and cook until the spices become aromatic.

Add the sweet potatoes and stir to coat, then pour in the stock and add the beans and peanut butter. Put a lid on the pot and cook for 10-15 minutes until the sweet potatoes are soft.

Remove the lid, mix in the spinach, and leave for 5 minutes until cooked through. Taste, then add salt until seasoned as you prefer.

Serve with boiled rice.

Ital
is Vital

Outside the hustle of Kingston, in the village of Papine, is a tiny restaurant. Fronted with wide bamboo, it is built out of concrete blocks painted the red, green, and gold of Ethiopia and Rastafari, and knocks out food so joyful it defies its modest exterior and diminutive size.

Shanty Man, an engaging figure with grey dreadlocks held up in a hair-wrap and a gentle smile across his face, has been here for years, serving his own brand of Ital food: fresh fruit juices, stews filled with a rainbow assortment of local vegetables, plates of ackee and plantain.

Little eateries such as Shanty Man's restaurant are dotted throughout Jamaica. They are founded in Rastafarianism but, thanks to their beautiful food and inspired methods—which largely avoid animal products and have natural produce at their core—have a much broader appeal.

The current wave of veganism in the West is distinguished by a booming trade in fake "meat" products and an explosion in "vegan junk food" that's a world away from the lentils-and-lettuce stereotype of the 1960s and 1970s.

105

But the Rastafari diet—Ital—places Jamaica's natural bounty front and center. There is no need for faking meat when good food made from fresh, local fruits and vegetables stands up all by itself. With ingredients of the quality that is on offer in Jamaica's markets, it's little wonder that this green island nation gave rise to such a phenomenal plant-based food culture, and one so closely rooted in the land.

The global perception of Rastafari as a belief is often reduced to tropes, namely dreadlocks, reggae, and ganja smoking. And while those elements have a role, Rastafarianism runs deep: it is both a spiritual belief system and a way of life in which the Ital diet is just one part. Other beliefs include the wearing of dreadlocks—in accordance with the teachings of Leviticus to "not make baldness upon their head"—and the ritualistic smoking of ganja, said to promote self-reflection and bring followers closer to Jah.

The roots of Rastafarianism lie in the social and economic legacy of slave society, followed by more than another century in Britain's colonial chains, which fomented a spirit of resistance in Jamaica. Born out of anti-imperialism and Black pride, it was the teachings of Marcus Garvey in the early 20th century that propelled it into a movement.

Born in St. Ann's in 1887, Garvey founded the Universal Negro Improvement Association (UNIA) in 1914 to promote racial pride and Black nationalism. He called for the return of the African diaspora to their ancestral homelands in Africa, a radical antidote to centuries of racial subjugation at the hands of the British and imperialist West. Garvey was a controversial and divisive figure, but his words resonated with many Black people, especially in the USA, where he gained a strong following in the poorer neighborhoods of the northern states.

In 1920, Garvey prophesied that a Black leader would be born who would realize the return to the promised land. The crowning of Tafari Makonnen (later known as Haile Selassie I) as the Emperor of Ethiopia just a decade later was perceived by many to be the realization of Garvey's prophecy. Garvey's followers believed Tafari to be the God of Ethiopia and the Second Coming of Christ. "Ras" means "head" or "prince," which, when added to "Tafari," gave the movement its name: Rastafari. Later, the songs of Rastafari's most famous son, Bob Marley, would propel the religion into the consciousness of millions and boost its following across the world.

At the core of the Rastafari religion is the concept of "livity," or life force. Everything is balanced. Food and drink, what we put in our body, is central to promoting livity. The term Ital is derived from "vital," placing emphasis on an individual's connection with nature: the Ital diet therefore is pure, organic, and natural. Food is medicine and medicine is food. In the same vein, Rastafari eschew Western medicines, preferring to heal themselves through natural remedies, a direct link to the Obeah men and women of the slave societies and their natural medicines, as well as Maroon communities and their ancient tradition of herbal therapies, such as fever grass (more commonly known as lemongrass) used to treat fevers.

There is no single definition of Ital food, although many Rastafari people avoid meat—especially pork—as well as animal products, though small fish are permitted. Processed foods and the use of additives and preservatives are often avoided, as is the use of salt with iodine; some people avoid salt completely. Instead, for seasoning, natural foods such as garlic, onion, pimento (allspice), and Scotch bonnet are used in abundance.

The recipes in this chapter follow the looser interpretation of Ital cooking, incorporating the beautiful produce of Jamaica, much of which is thankfully available outside the island and online. In Europe, the Mediterranean diet is lauded for its health, but, for me, the Caribbean diet is a brilliant example of vibrant living and, within that, pared-back yet delicious Ital food is one of the simplest and tastiest ways to eat.

Jaxx and me at a fruit stall on the way to Boston

SEASONED CALLALOO

When I traveled to Jamaica to research this book, in summer 2021, I stayed at Tranquility Estate, a boutique B&B in Kingston, in the foothills of the Blue Mountains. It's run by Lorna, the mother of my friend Jaxx, and I couldn't have stayed in a more beautiful place. Every morning I'd wake up and watch the sun rise above the tree-blanketed hills that surrounded me. I thought the mornings couldn't get better, until Lorna made me breakfast of ackee and saltfish with all the trimmings, including boiled dumpling, hard food, and this seasoned callaloo. She sent me the recipe and permitted me to include it here. It's incredible.

SERVES 4–6 AS A SIDE

3 tbsp vegetable oil
1 large onion, chopped
1 lb (500 g) callaloo, roughly chopped
    (or you can use kale or mature spinach),
    coarse stalks removed
2 tomatoes, chopped
½ red bell pepper, sliced
2 tbsp dried mixed herbs
    (Badia is a great brand)
leaves from 1 thyme sprig
4 tbsp water
½ tsp sea salt

Heat the oil in a frying pan and cook the onion over medium heat. Once it's softened, add the rest of the ingredients (unless you are using spinach, in which case reserve that for now) and cook for about 10 minutes so the callaloo (or kale) is cooked through.

If you are using spinach, add this now, once the rest of the ingredients are cooked: take the pan off the heat with a lid on and the residual heat will cook it through. As soon as that has happened, serve.

SMOKY EGGPLANT RUNDOWN

This is a vegan version of my Smoked Mackerel Rundown (see page 59) and it is immense. The eggplant is smoky and sweet and the creamy coconut just makes every mouthful a delight.

SERVES 4

4-6 eggplants
1 onion, sliced
vegetable oil
3 garlic cloves, crushed
1 in (2.5 cm) piece of ginger, grated
1 red bell pepper, sliced
7 oz (200 g) yellow yam or pumpkin, peeled,
    deseeded if needed, and chopped
2 tomatoes, chopped
3 thyme sprigs
½ tsp ground pimento (allspice)
½ tsp ground cumin
14 oz (400 g) can of coconut milk
    (for homemade, see page 271)
2 bay leaves

To serve
Fried Dumpling, Lorna's Boiled Dumpling,
    or Boiled Green Bananas (see pages 224
    and 227)

Grill the eggplants whole over a naked flame—either on a gas stove or on the grill—until the flesh is just soft, the skin is burnt, and the air smells smoky. Place in a lidded container and, once cool enough to handle, peel. If you don't have a flame, you can cook them under the broiler until they start to smoke, or even do it in a dry pan over high heat, turning frequently to blister the skin. Once peeled, roughly chop into big chunks.

Fry the onion in a splash of oil in a large frying pan for 5 minutes until it starts to soften. Add the garlic, ginger, red pepper, yam or pumpkin, tomatoes, and thyme and fry for another 5 minutes, then add the spices and fry until they are aromatic. Pour in the coconut milk and add the bay leaves. Add a splash of water to loosen, put a lid on it, and cook down for 15-20 minutes, until the pumpkin or yam has softened.

Remove the lid, stir in the eggplants, and cook for another 8 minutes until the sauce has thickened. Pick out the thyme sprigs, if you want. Serve with Fried Dumpling, Lorna's Boiled Dumpling, or Boiled Green Bananas.

ITAL STEW

This is probably the most common Ital dish found in Jamaica. It comes in various combinations, depending on what is available, but always celebrates vegetables in their purest form.

This is my version, and once you are familiar with the recipe you can play around with it and use vegetables that are abundant where you live. Carrots, breadfruit, gungo peas, black-eyed peas, dasheen (taro), and different varieties of yam also work well.

Strict followers of Rastafari will avoid the use of salt, preferring to rely on the natural flavorings instead. I'll leave that for you to decide.

SERVES 4-6

2 tbsp coconut oil, or vegetable oil
1 onion, chopped
3 garlic cloves, crushed
2 in (5 cm) piece of ginger, grated
3 scallions, chopped
3 thyme sprigs
1 red bell pepper, cut into cubes
1 tsp ground turmeric
14 oz (400 ml) can of coconut milk
    (for homemade, see page 271)
scant 1 cup (200 ml) water
1 medium potato, peeled and cut into cubes
2 ears of corn, each cut into 4 rounds
5½ oz (150 g) pumpkin, peeled, deseeded,
    and cut into cubes
1 chocho (chayote), peeled, deseeded, and
    cut into cubes
1 sweet potato, peeled and cut into cubes
2 bunches of callaloo (or use mature
    bunches of spinach instead), coarse
    stalks removed, roughly chopped
sea salt (optional)
Rice & Peas, to serve (see page 231)

In a Dutch pot or heavy-based pot, heat the oil over medium heat and cook the onion for 5 minutes before adding the garlic, ginger, scallions, thyme sprigs, and red pepper.

Cook for 5 minutes until everything is softening together, then stir in the turmeric, coconut milk, measured water, potato, corn, and pumpkin. Cook for 10 minutes and then add the rest of the vegetables apart from the callaloo.

Bring to a boil, then reduce the heat and simmer for 20 minutes until the vegetables are tender and the sauce has thickened, adding the callaloo when there are 10 minutes left; it should be very soft. Pick out the thyme sprigs and season with salt, if you want.

Serve with Rice & Peas.

RED PEAS SOUP

Red peas, or kidney beans, are a staple in Jamaica. Red Peas Soup is ubiquitous on the island, often with bits of stewed beef found hiding at the bottom. I always burn myself eating it because I'm too impatient to let it cool down.

This version is vegan, and for me it's as lovely as the meaty alternative. It's packed full of flavor and the beans give it a lovely thickness. If you avoid soups as a meal because you find them lacking, give this one a try.

SERVES 4-6

6⅓ cups (1.5 liters) water
1⅔ cups (300 g) dried kidney beans,
    soaked overnight
3 thyme sprigs
2 onions, chopped
1 garlic clove, very finely chopped
2 carrots, roughly chopped
2 tsp all-purpose seasoning
10½ oz (300 g) yam, peeled and cut into
    ½ in (1 cm) cubes
2 potatoes, peeled and cut into ¾ in
    (2 cm) cubes
scant 1 cup (200 ml) coconut milk
    (for homemade, see page 271)
pinch of sea salt
Spinners, to serve (optional, see page 228)

Bring the measured water to a boil in a large pot or stockpot, then reduce the heat to a simmer. Drain the soaked kidney beans, tip them into the pot with the thyme, and cook until tender, 1–1½ hours.

Add the onion and garlic, cook for 10 minutes, then add all the remaining ingredients apart from the coconut milk and salt, and cook until the vegetables are tender but not too soft, 10–15 minutes. If you want Spinners in the soup, add them to cook as on page 228, 5 minutes after the yam and potatoes go in.

Season with a pinch of salt and pick out the thyme sprigs, if you want. Stir in the coconut milk and serve.

THYME-ROASTED TOMATOES

These tomatoes are simplicity personified but are really good as a side, especially to Macaroni Cheese (see page 192). They make the most of tomatoes from colder climates that aren't so naturally sweet; roasting draws out their sweetness and makes them burst with flavor. Made in bigger quantities and blended, they also make a great sauce.

SERVES 4–6 AS A SIDE

8 tomatoes
oil (I use canola or olive oil)
4 thyme sprigs
1 tsp sea salt, or Thyme Salt (see below)
freshly ground black pepper

Preheat the oven to 350°F (180°C).

Cut the tomatoes in half horizontally and lay them on a baking tray lined with parchment paper, cut sides up.

Drizzle with oil and gently rub it in so the surfaces are covered. Scrape the thyme sprigs with your hands over the tomatoes so the leaves drop on the surfaces, then drop the stalks on top too. Sprinkle salt or Thyme Salt and pepper over them and place in the oven.

Roast for 30 minutes, then serve.

THYME SALT

This is a brilliant way to get extra flavor into a dish alongside other seasoning. It's easy to make and now sits on my countertop alongside my regular sea salt flakes. I use it all the time. It's great as a base for dishes, adding a hit of extra flavor to them even in those where I wouldn't usually add thyme, and works as a flavor in its own right, such as with the tomatoes above or with Cassava Fries (see page 220).

MAKES ABOUT 3½ OZ (100 G)

1¾ oz (50 g) thyme leaves and thin stalks
   (preferably woody thyme, rather than
   the softer, plastic-packaged thyme found
   in most supermarkets)
2½ tbsp (50 g) coarse sea salt

Carefully rinse the thyme, trying not to lose too many leaves in the process. Leave it to dry on a sheet of paper towel. Once dry, transfer to a plate and leave in a warm place for 2 days until the leaves dry out.

Blend in a spice grinder or a mortar and pestle with the salt and transfer to a clean, dry glass jar. It'll keep for ages, but try to use it within 3 months. That shouldn't be too much of a problem...

PLANTAIN & GUNGO PEA BUN

Every bite of this bun brings something a bit different, whether sweet from the plantain or earthy from the peas. I serve this in Coco Bread (see page 236) in a sort of Sloppy Joe style, but the plantain and gungo pea mixture is also excellent with plain boiled rice. Real comfort.

SERVES 6-8

½ red onion, finely chopped
vegetable oil
2 garlic cloves, crushed
½–¾ in (1½–2 cm) piece of ginger,
    finely grated
5 scallions, finely chopped
2 ripe but firm plantain, chopped into
    ½ in (1 cm) cubes
1 tsp ground pimento (allspice)
1 tsp freshly ground black pepper
3 tomatoes, chopped
14 oz (400 g) can of gungo peas, drained
⅔ cup (150 ml) coconut milk
    (for homemade, see page 271)
sea salt

To serve
Coco Bread (see page 236), or plain rice

Fry the onion in a splash of oil. After 5 minutes, add the garlic, ginger, and 3 of the scallions. Cook for a couple of minutes, then add the plantain. You may need another splash of oil. Keep moving the plantain pieces so they get color all over, then add the pimento, pepper, and some salt. Cook out for a couple of minutes, then add the tomatoes.

Cook for a couple of minutes, then add the gungo peas and coconut milk. Cook it down so the sauce is really thick, about 8 minutes.

Just before serving, stir in the remaining 2 scallions. Serve stuffed into Coco Bread (to keep it vegan, swap dairy butter for a plant-based alternative in the bread recipe), or with plain rice.

STEAMED CABBAGE

Simple to make, and totally worth it. Steamed cabbage is a classic Jamaican dish, either served as a side—it's great with Fried Fish (see page 76)—or it is more than tasty enough to eat on its own with boiled rice.

SERVES 4 AS A SIDE

1 tbsp vegetable oil
1 onion, finely sliced
2 garlic cloves, crushed
½ red or orange bell pepper, finely sliced
leaves from 2 thyme sprigs
1 medium carrot, cut into matchsticks
1 Scotch bonnet
½ tsp sea salt
1 small cabbage, core removed, shredded
scant ½ cup (100 ml) vegetable stock
   (for homemade, see page 127)

Heat the oil in a frying pan over medium heat. Cook the onion for a couple of minutes, then add the garlic, pepper, thyme, carrot, Scotch bonnet, and salt. Cook for another couple of minutes—being careful to not color the onion—and then add the cabbage.

Mix well, pour in the stock and cover. Cook for 5 minutes until the cabbage is tender, then serve, picking out the whole Scotch bonnet, if using, or warning your guests not to eat it!

YAM & GUNGO PEAS STEW

A really warming, hearty plateful, this is one of my favorite dishes. As a kid I didn't like yam, but I had to eat it anyway. Nowadays I can't get enough of it. It's the texture for me, especially in soups and stews where it gives the most satisfying chew.

SERVES 4-6

3½ oz (100 g) dried gungo peas, soaked
   overnight
2 onions, chopped
1 tbsp vegetable oil
4 garlic cloves, crushed
2 in (5 cm) piece of ginger, finely grated
4 thyme sprigs
1 tsp ground pimento (allspice)
½ tsp ground cumin
½ tsp ground coriander
12½ oz (350 g) yam, peeled and chopped
1 carrot, chopped
1 Scotch bonnet (optional)
scant 1 cup (200 ml) vegetable stock
   (for homemade, see page 127)
scant 1 cup (200 ml) coconut milk
   (for homemade, see page 271)
sea salt and freshly ground black pepper

To serve
Lorna's Boiled Dumpling, Boiled Green
   Bananas, or plain rice (see page 227)

Put the drained gungo peas in a pot of water and cook for 1–1½ hours until soft and tender. Drain and set aside.

Fry the onions in the oil for 8 minutes until soft. Add the garlic, ginger, thyme, pimento, cumin, and coriander and cook until the spices become aromatic.

Add the yam, carrot ,and Scotch bonnet, if using, either whole for flavor or finely chop ¼–½ of it for heat. Mix, then pour in the vegetable stock and coconut milk. Bring to a boil, then reduce the heat and cook for 15 minutes until the vegetables are soft. Taste and season with salt and pepper. Add the gungo peas and cook for a final 10 minutes, tasting and seasoning again. Pick out the thyme sprigs, if you want, and whole Scotch bonnet, if using.

Serve with Lorna's Boiled Dumpling, Boiled Green Bananas, or plain rice.

APPLE COLESLAW

Coleslaw is a great foil for spicy food. In summer 2021, I cooked at Meatopia, a live-fire-cooking festival in London, alongside Maureen Tyne (see pages 182 and 278). Our Meatopia dish was Jerk Pork with Pepper Sauce (see pages 157 and 278). The apple in the coleslaw was Maureen's idea and I love the crisp freshness of it, while the pairing of apple with pork gives it a decidedly British feel too.

SERVES 6 AS A SIDE

½ white cabbage, very finely shredded
¼ red cabbage, very finely shredded
1 red onion, sliced as finely as possible
1 carrot, cut into fine matchsticks
2 tart apples (such as Granny Smith),
    cut into fine matchsticks
juice of ½ lemon
1 tsp sea salt

For the dressing
3 tbsp mayonnaise, or vegan mayonnaise
    if required
2 tbsp plain yogurt, or plant-based yogurt
    if required
2 tbsp apple cider vinegar

Mix all the vegetables and apples together in a big bowl. Separately mix the dressing ingredients, then combine them with the vegetables and lemon juice.

Season with salt just before serving. If you're making this ahead of time, leave out the salt until it's ready to be served, so it doesn't draw out the liquid from the vegetables and fruit and make the coleslaw soggy.

(Pictured on page 150)

VEGETABLE STOCK

Homemade stocks are great on so many levels. They help to reduce food waste, they taste great, and you can control what you put in them.

Keep a bag in the freezer for all the peelings and trimmed ends of the vegetables listed below. Avoid anything from starchy vegetables such as potato, sweet potato, yam, or cassava, or brassicas such as cabbage, cauliflower, and broccoli, as the latter release an unpleasant taste once cooked down for a long time. (Just think of the smell of cabbage boiled to mush.)

Add vegetables that are past their best though, salvaging what you can before throwing unusable bits away. Mushroom stalks that are too woody to eat are a good addition, as are herbs such as thyme and parsley. Remember, any strong-tasting herb will affect the flavor of the stock, so avoid those such as tarragon, dill, and fennel unless you are happy for the stock to take on those flavors.

I don't add salt to my stock, so I can control how much salt is in the final dish by tasting as I cook.

MAKES 2 CUPS (500 ML)

Include any of:
carrot, celery, garlic, leek, mushroom, onion, parsley, shallot, scallion

Include in small quantities, towards the end of cooking:
eggplant, zucchini, lettuce, peppers, deseeded tomato

Avoid:
beet, broccoli, cabbage, cassava, cauliflower, chocho (chayote), potato, pumpkin, squash, sweet potato, strong-tasting herbs (unless you want the stock to taste like the herb), yam

Always include:
bay leaf, black peppercorns, thyme sprigs

Collect off-cuts of any of the vegetables listed to the left, even those that are past their best, adding any non-strong-tasting herbs that are wilted. Keep in a bag in the freezer and once you have enough, make stock.

Weigh the freezer bag, then empty the contents into a large pot with a bay leaf, a small handful of peppercorns, and some thyme sprigs. Pour in 4¼ cups (1 liter) of water for each 5½ oz (150 g) of vegetables. Bring to a boil, then reduce the heat to a simmer and cook for 1 hour.

Strain the stock into a bowl and either use it straight away or freeze. If freezer space is limited, reduce the stock to a concentrated liquid, freeze it in an ice cube tray and use as "stock cubes."

Yard Birds

Chickens run free in Jamaica, a nod to historic days when they would meander around the streets pecking for bits to eat.

Relatively inexpensive, chicken is a ubiquitous feature on menus, from jerk chicken—now the most popular way to eat jerk, having overtaken pork—to brown stew chicken and fried chicken. KFC is the island's most popular takeout; the only McDonald's branch in Jamaica closed after a decade, due to lack of demand.

Chicken feet make it into soup, while the island also imports tons of chicken backs, an inexpensive way to get a bit of extra flavor and protein into stews and soups.

You'll also find here a recipe for roast chicken with grapefruit and thyme; it's a stunning dish, perfect for lazy Sundays. The carcass makes beautifully flavored stock for soup, too.

Boston jerk centre

STICKY RUM & TAMARIND WINGS

Jamaican rum is a great ingredient in cooking. It adds depth and a complexity to flavors, especially when paired with Tamarind Brown Sauce (see page 279).

These wings are really delicious and easy to make, you can even bake them if you don't fancy deep-frying. The marinade and sauce can be used with cauliflower too, for a vegan alternative; just swap out the honey for agave syrup and make the vegan version of Tamarind Brown Sauce.

SERVES 4

16 chicken wings
1¼ cups (150 g) all-purpose flour
    (I sometimes use potato starch/flour
    since it's gluten-free, or cornstarch would
    be fine too)
vegetable oil, for deep-frying or brushing,
    to taste
2 scallions, chopped (optional)
½ Scotch bonnet, deseeded and finely
    chopped (optional)
sea salt and freshly ground black pepper

For the marinade
⅓ cup (75 ml) soy sauce
3 in (7.5 cm) piece of ginger, finely grated
3 garlic cloves, crushed
1 tsp sea salt
1 tsp freshly ground black pepper

For the sauce
5 tbsp Tamarind Brown Sauce (see page 279)
1 garlic clove, grated
2 tbsp dark rum
up to 2 tbsp Pepper Sauce, to taste
    (see page 278)
1½ tbsp apple cider vinegar
1 tbsp soy sauce
2 tbsp honey

Remove the wing tips and add to your freezer chicken stock bag (see page 138). Place the rest of the wings in a large bowl.

Mix all the marinade ingredients and add to the wings. Cover and leave in the fridge for at least 4 hours, or overnight.

Preheat the oven to 320°F (160°C) and line a large baking sheet with parchment paper.

Put the flour in a large bowl, season it well with salt and pepper, then toss the wings to coat. Once completely covered, place on the prepared baking sheet.

Bake for 15 minutes, or, if using large wings, up to 20 minutes. Remove the baking sheet from the oven and allow to cool.

Meanwhile, following all the usual precautions for deep-frying (see page 288), heat the oil in a pot until it reaches 350°F (180°C); if you don't have a thermometer, this is when a pinch of flour starts bubbling after 2 seconds. Fry the wings in batches, so as not to overcrowd the pan, for 5 minutes, then drain on a wire rack set over paper towels to catch the oil.

Alternatively, if you don't want to deep-fry, increase the oven temperature to 400°F (200°C), brush the wings with oil, and return to the oven for 6 minutes, until golden and crispy.

Put all the sauce ingredients in a wide sauté pan and set over medium-high heat until it starts to bubble. Add the wings and toss, so they're all covered. If the sauce reduces too much, add a dash of water. Once the sauce has reduced and is sticky, remove from the heat and plate up. Sprinkle with scallions and Scotch bonnet, if you like, and enjoy!

GRANDMA'S CURRY CHICKEN

My grandma Catherine was a brilliant cook and this was her signature dish. The family remains obsessed by it; my uncle Nigel even once won a television cooking show with this on his menu.

It was the one dish I asked Grandma to show me how to cook. I couldn't have been older than 10, but I still remember everything about it. The measurements were loose; it was all done by eye, but it was always excellent.

Although I was shown how to make this, it still took me a long time to perfect the recipe and get it like Grandma's. I think she used an all-purpose seasoning with MSG in it, which is why it had a lovely umami pepperiness to it, and you've *got* to fry the chicken in butter. Cut no corners.

SERVES 4

1 whole chicken, cut into 10 pieces (see page 145, but don't cut the drumsticks and thighs in half)
1 onion, finely sliced
3 garlic cloves, crushed
2 tbsp Jamaican curry powder (for homemade, see page 23)
1 tbsp all-purpose seasoning (ideally containing MSG)
2 tbsp vegetable oil, plus more if needed
2 tbsp salted butter
2 tomatoes, chopped
2 bay leaves
2 cups (500 ml) water
1 chicken or vegetable stock cube

To serve
Rice & Peas or Festival (see pages 231 and 223)

In a large bowl, mix the chicken pieces with the onion, garlic, curry powder, and all-purpose seasoning. Cover and leave for 2 hours in the fridge.

In a large pot, heat the oil over medium heat. Add the butter and then a few of the chicken pieces, scraping off and reserving the bits of onion. Make sure the chicken is in a single layer and that the pieces are not touching.

Fry for 5 minutes until browned on all sides. Transfer to a bowl and repeat with the remaining chicken pieces until they are all browned.

Return the pot to the heat. Add more oil if needed and then fry the onion from the marinade for 8 minutes until soft. Return the chicken pieces to the pot with the tomatoes and bay leaves and mix well. Add the measured water, crumble in the stock cube, and cook for 40–50 minutes.

Serve with Rice & Peas, made with kidney beans, or Festival.

CHICKEN CORN SOUP

I'm not a huge soup lover—usually I find them too light and lacking in substance to fill me up—unless we're talking Jamaican soups. Jamaican soups are something else. The complete contents of a Jamaican soup pot are often a mystery; it only reveals its delights the deeper you get. Hard food? Spinners? Chicken feet?

This is my chicken soup, how I like it. It's not bolstered with any packaged soup mix (such as Grace soup mix), though you can add that if you like towards the end of cooking time and adjust the seasoning accordingly (you'll need less salt).

SERVES 4

½ chicken on the bone (any combination:
   2 whole legs, or 2 breasts and wings, or
   1 leg and 1 breast and wing...)
8½ cups (2 liters) light chicken stock
   (for homemade, see page 138)
2 carrots, halved lengthways, then sliced
1 onion, chopped
7 oz (200 g) pumpkin or butternut squash,
   peeled, deseeded, and cubed
7 oz (200 g) yam, peeled and chopped
2 celery sticks, chopped
1 cup (150 g) corn kernels, or 2 ears of corn
   each cut into 3–4 rings
1 tsp dried mixed herbs
   (Badia is a great brand)
1 garlic clove, crushed
2 scallions, white parts only,
   finely chopped
1 tsp freshly ground white pepper, or
   freshly ground black pepper
1 tbsp all-purpose flour
sea salt
Spinners, to serve (see page 228)

Make sure the chicken is portioned up into drumsticks and thighs, or breasts cut into 3 on the bone (or do it yourself, see page 145). Bring a large pot of water to a boil, add the chicken, and leave for 1 minute. Remove the chicken and rinse it to remove any scum, then discard the cooking water. Wipe the pot clean.

Bring the stock to a boil in the cleaned pot. Add the chicken and reduce the heat to a simmer. Cook for 10 minutes, then add the carrots, onion, pumpkin, yam, celery, corn, dried herbs, garlic, scallions, and pepper. Cook for 20 minutes, then remove the chicken and leave to cool. Leave the soup simmering.

Put the flour in a small bowl and mix in a ladleful of soup. Once mixed, return it to the soup pot and stir until thickened.

Add the Spinners to cook as on page 228.

Shred the cooled chicken pieces and return the meat to the soup, then serve.

CHICKEN STOCK

A decent chicken stock will elevate your food. You cannot make a decent gravy without it and it's worth making from scratch. I always keep a bag of chicken bones in the freezer—chicken carcasses and backbones, thigh bones after making Curry Fried Chicken, wing tips after making Sticky Rum & Tamarind Wings (see pages 142 and 132), chicken necks, and so on. A lot of butchers sell bones now too, in a bag, for a couple of dollars. Roasting them gives a depth of flavor, or leave them unroasted for a lighter broth.

MAKES ABOUT 3 CUPS (750 ML)

4½ lb (2 kg) chicken bones
a little white wine vinegar, or apple
    cider vinegar
2 carrots, chopped
2 celery sticks, chopped
2 onions, chopped
3 scallions, chopped
1 garlic bulb, cloves separated and peeled
oil
handful of thyme sprigs
1 tbsp dried pimento (allspice) berries
1 tbsp black peppercorns
sea salt

Preheat the oven to 350°F (180°C). Wash the bones in a large bowl in the sink, with water and the vinegar (see page 288).

Empty the bones into an ovenproof dish, add half the vegetables and garlic, and coat with a splash of oil. Add a sprinkle of salt and bake for 30 minutes.

Transfer to a large pot with the remaining ingredients and fill with water so the ingredients are well submerged.

Bring to a boil, then reduce the heat to a simmer, skimming off any scum. Let it blip away for 2 hours, then turn the heat off and let it steep for 1 hour before straining.

Taste and add more salt if necessary.

Use as is, or freeze. If freezer space is limited, reduce the stock to a concentrated liquid, freeze it in an ice cube tray, and use as "stock cubes."

PROPER CHICKEN GRAVY

Dunking a piece of Proper Fried Chicken (see overleaf) into Proper Chicken Gravy brings a taste of comfort like no other. It's a rare treat, not an everyday occurrence, so I like to do it—well—properly. This gravy also goes well with Roast Chicken with Thyme & Grapefruit (see page 146).

MAKES 2–2⅓ CUPS (500–550 ML)

3½ tbsp (50 g) unsalted butter
6 tbsp (50 g) all-purpose flour
   (or cornstarch, to keep
   it gluten-free)
3 cups (750 ml) Chicken Stock (see opposite;
   I'm afraid it has to be homemade here)
sea salt

Melt the butter in a pot, stir in the flour, and cook over medium heat until medium brown and nutty, 6–8 minutes. If you're using cornstarch it won't color much, but cook it out for the same amount of time.

Slowly stir in the stock bit by bit, ensuring each addition is fully incorporated before pouring in the next. Once it is all added, cook the gravy down to the desired consistency. Season with salt, then serve just before eating.

JERK CHICKEN GRAVY

Just a tweaked version of the recipe above, but vital as a side to Jerk Chicken (see page 148).

MAKES 500–550ML

2 tbsp leftover jerk marinade (see page 148)
3½ tbsp (50 g) unsalted butter
6 tbsp (50 g) all-purpose flour
3 cups (750 ml) Chicken Stock (see opposite)
3 tbsp ketchup
1 tsp honey (optional)
1 tsp sea salt (optional)

Put the jerk marinade and butter into a pot and fry for 5 minutes. Then add the flour and mix well.

Gradually add the stock, incorporating each bit completely before adding the next.

Now add the ketchup and cook until the gravy thickens. Taste, then add honey and salt, if you like.

PROPER FRIED CHICKEN

Fried chicken is, to me, the purest and tastiest comfort food known. That is why it's made its way around the world, with nearly every nation having their own iteration of floured or battered chicken fried in oil. It's on most menus in Jamaica, whether at a patty shop or restaurant. And it's a commonly held belief that Jamaican KFC is the best in the world. I couldn't possibly comment, having not sampled every nation's version, though I agree that it is very good. Just not as good as Tastee's in Papine.

Proper fried chicken takes time, to layer up flavor. Relying on the coating alone isn't enough. Brining chicken—or any meat—enhances flavor and tenderizes it. The salt solution passes into the chicken, along with any aromatics you add. And the salt relaxes the protein in the meat, making it tender and juicy.

Most fried chicken in Jamaica won't be brined. But this recipe is my ultimate version, honed over years of making a lot of it. It's not an everyday dish, but a special occasion meal, which is why I put so much effort in.

It sits alongside my Curry Fried Chicken (see overleaf), which is a homage to my love of Grandma's Curry Chicken (see page 135), in fried form. Both recipes are very close to my heart and I hope you enjoy them.

SERVES 4

1 whole chicken, cut into 8-10 pieces
    (see page 145, but don't cut the drumsticks
    and thighs in half), skin on
1⅔ cups (200 g) all-purpose flour
1 tsp all-purpose seasoning
1 tsp dried thyme
1 tsp freshly ground black pepper
1 tsp paprika
1 tsp garlic powder
1 tsp onion powder (optional)
vegetable oil, for deep-frying

For the brine
8½ cups (2 liters) water
4 tbsp (80 g) coarse sea salt
8 dried pimento (allspice) berries
4 garlic cloves, lightly bruised
3 in (7.5 cm) piece of ginger, sliced
1 lime, sliced
1 tbsp black peppercorns
3 scallions, sliced

To serve
Proper Chicken Gravy (see page 139)

For the brine, heat 1 cup (250 ml) of the measured water and dissolve the salt in it. Add the rest of the brine ingredients along with the remaining 7½ cups (1.75 liters) water. Turn off the heat and leave until the brine is completely cold. Put the chicken pieces in the brine, in a large container that will fit in your fridge, so they are completely submerged. Refrigerate for 24 hours.

Drain the chicken. Mix the flour with the all-purpose seasoning, thyme, black pepper, paprika, garlic powder, and onion powder (if using) in a large bowl. Drop the chicken in, a couple of pieces at a time. Mix them around to ensure they are fully covered in the flour, getting it on every bit of surface. Continue to coat all the chicken, then rest them on a plate for 10 minutes.

Following all the usual precautions for deep-frying (see page 288), heat the oil in a large pot to 300°F (150°C); if you haven't got an oil thermometer, drop a piece of bread into the oil and it should sink and then start to bubble and rise after 4-5 seconds.

Fry the chicken, in batches so as not to overcrowd the pan, for 15 minutes, then remove to a wire rack placed over paper towels, to soak up the oil. Repeat until all the chicken has had its first fry.

Heat the oil up to 350°F/180°C (see page 288), then return the chicken pieces, again in batches, for a second fry, this time for 3 minutes so they crisp up and turn golden.

Serve with Proper Chicken Gravy.

CURRY FRIED CHICKEN (CFC)

This dish is the culmination of my deep love of two things: fried chicken and curry chicken. The addition of coconut milk really brings everything together, enriching the flavors while also mellowing them. And although I would always usually choose chicken on the bone, this works better with boneless thighs.

SERVES 4

6 skinless, boneless chicken thighs
2 tbsp Jamaican curry powder
 (for homemade, see page 23)
3 garlic cloves, crushed
2 in (5 cm) piece of ginger, finely grated
leaves from 3 thyme sprigs
1½ tsp sea salt
⅔ cup (150 ml) coconut milk
 (for homemade, see page 271)
vegetable oil, for deep-frying
freshly ground black pepper

For the coating
scant 1 cup (100 g) potato starch/flour,
 or all-purpose flour
⅔ cup (100 g) fine cornmeal
1 tsp sea salt
1 tsp ground ginger
1 tsp ground cumin
1 tsp ground turmeric

For the chile and lime mayo
4 tbsp store-bought mayonnaise
finely grated zest and juice of 1 lime
¼ Scotch bonnet, finely chopped

To serve (all optional)
1 Scotch bonnet, sliced widthways into rings
boiled rice
Coco Bread (see page 236)
Pepper Sauce Mayo (see page 47)

Cut each thigh into 2–3 pieces, each about 1½ in (4 cm) big. Put the pieces in a bowl with the curry powder and mix well. Add the garlic, ginger, thyme, salt, and a pinch of pepper and mix well, then add the coconut milk and mix to coat completely. Cover and marinate for at least 4 hours in the fridge, but ideally overnight.

To make the coating, mix the potato starch or flour, cornmeal, salt, and spices in a bowl. Remove the chicken from the marinade, scraping off any big bits but otherwise leaving everything where it is, and place in the flour mixture.

Turn the pieces over and press down, ensuring every nook and cranny is exposed to the flour. Remove and rest on a plate for at least 5 minutes, giving the starch enough time to adhere to the chicken.

Mix together all the ingredients for the mayo in a small bowl.

Set up a wire rack over a tray lined with paper towels. Following all the usual precautions for deep-frying (see page 288), pour enough oil into a pot to lie at least 4 in (10 cm) deep. Heat it to about 285°F (140°C). If you don't have a thermometer, a sprinkling of flour should sizzle gently a few seconds after being dropped into it.

Place a few pieces of chicken into the oil, making sure you don't crowd them. Fry for 3–4 minutes, until they start to color, then remove with a slotted spoon and transfer to the wire rack. Continue until every piece has had its first fry.

Now increase the oil temperature to 350°F/180°C (see page 288), or until a pinch of flour sizzles almost immediately on contact with the oil.

Add the chicken pieces, starting with those that went first into the oil before. Fry for a further 2 minutes or until they have turned a deeper golden brown and are crisp. Remove and drain on the rack, continuing until all pieces have been fried twice.

Fry the Scotch bonnet rings for a minute or so, then drain on the rack.

Serve the chicken with a sprinkling of fried chile on top, with the chile and lime mayo and rice, or enjoy in Coco Bread with a smear of Pepper Sauce Mayo.

BROWN STEW CHICKEN

A classic recipe across the Caribbean, especially in Jamaica. It gets its name and color from the browning, a mix of browned sugar and vegetable stock. This dish means comfort to me and it's a meal I always come back to.

SERVES 4

3 lb 5 oz (1.5 kg) whole chicken
1½ tsp sea salt
1 tsp freshly ground black pepper
1 large onion, finely sliced
3 garlic cloves, crushed
2 in (5 cm) piece of ginger, finely grated
3 thyme sprigs
1 tbsp ground pimento (allspice)
1 tbsp all-purpose seasoning
2 scallions, roughly chopped
1 tbsp Savory Browning (see page 275)
3 tbsp vegetable oil
1 red bell pepper, sliced
1¼ cups (300 ml) water
2 tbsp soft light brown sugar
1 tbsp soy sauce
2 tbsp ketchup
1 Scotch bonnet

To serve
Rice & Peas or Roasted Breadfruit and
    Steamed Cabbage (see pages 231,
    219, and 123)

Cut the chicken into small pieces: separate the drumsticks and thighs and cut both in half using a cleaver. Divide each breast, on the bone, into 3–4 pieces. Separate the wings into the drum and flat. Remove the skin from every piece apart from the wings and freeze it for stock, along with the wing tips and backbone.

Mix the chicken pieces in a bowl with the salt, pepper, onion, garlic, ginger, thyme, pimento, all-purpose seasoning, scallions, and Savory Browning. Leave to marinate for at least 4 hours in the fridge, ideally overnight.

Put the oil in a Dutch pot or heavy-based pot. Scrape as much of the marinade off the chicken pieces back into the bowl as you can (reserve this) and brown the chicken on all sides, in batches if needed, so as not to overcrowd the pot.

Transfer the chicken to a plate and scrape the marinade into the pot. Cook for 10 minutes over medium-high heat until the onion starts to color, then add the red pepper. Mix well and return the chicken to the pot with the measured water and all the remaining ingredients. Include the Scotch bonnet whole for flavor, or finely chop ¼–½ of it for heat.

Bring to a boil, then reduce the heat to a simmer. Cook for 25 minutes until the sauce is thick, dark, and glossy and the chicken is cooked through. Pick out the thyme sprigs, if you want, and the whole Scotch bonnet, if using.

Serve with Rice & Peas or Roasted Breadfruit and Steamed Cabbage.

ROAST CHICKEN WITH THYME & GRAPEFRUIT

When I first went to Jamaica, I ate the best grapefruit of my life. It was a bit sour, but also really sweet and just beautifully fragrant. I smuggled about four into my luggage and savored them back in the cold UK.

I think grapefruit are criminally underused, so I use them as often as I can. We all love citrus with chicken, but a more unusual combination with grapefruit is excellent. If you can't get hold of Jamaican grapefruit, I'd use a combination of yellow and pink grapefruit, which will be pretty much exactly right.

SERVES 4-6

5 tbsp (70 g) salted butter, at room
   temperature
2 garlic cloves, crushed
1 shallot, finely chopped
1 tsp freshly ground black pepper
1 scallion, finely chopped
1 tsp thyme leaves
1 tsp sea salt
1 grapefruit, zested and quartered
1 whole chicken, at room temperature
olive oil, or canola oil
2 tbsp all-purpose flour, or cornstarch to
   keep the dish gluten-free
sea salt

To serve (optional)
plain rice or roast yam and mixed vegetables

Mix the butter, garlic, shallot, pepper, scallion, thyme, salt, and grapefruit zest until fully combined. Preheat the oven to 400°F (200°C).

Lay the chicken on a roasting pan and, starting at the rear end, carefully slide your hand under the breast skin to separate it from the flesh. Use your fingers to gently prize it apart, trying not to tear it. Go as far as you can, including over the legs; more separation means more space for butter, but don't force it. Take a small handful of seasoned butter and push it in the gap. Keep going; push it into every space until it is used up.

Push the zested grapefruit quarters into the cavity, squeezing them as you go to release the juice, which will steam as the chicken cooks and help to scent the inside.

Drizzle the chicken with oil, rubbing it in to cover the bird all over including the legs and wings, then sprinkle with sea salt flakes. Be careful to not move the chicken too much as that could mean you lose the grapefruit juice inside.

Roast for 10 minutes. Reduce the oven temperature to 320°F (160°C) and cook for a further 35–50 minutes depending on the size of the bird. If you have a meat thermometer, stick it into the thickest part of the chicken, such as where the thigh joins the body. Once it reads 165°F (70°C), the chicken is cooked. Otherwise stick a skewer into the same place and check the juices run clear. Remove from the oven.

Using a pair of tongs and a fork, remove the grapefruit quarters and squeeze to extract any extra juice before discarding. Carefully lift out the chicken, angling it so the juices pour out into the roasting pan. Place the chicken on a dish to rest.

Scrape the roasting pan to loosen any stuck-on bits, then strain the juices into a jug through a sieve. Take off as much of the fat that has risen to the top as you can and put it in a saucepan over medium heat. Add the flour or cornstarch and mix to form a smooth paste. Cook for 5 minutes, then gradually add the juices, stirring. Add splashes of water if needed to get a consistency you want, and taste for seasoning.

Serve with plain rice or roast yam, the gravy, and mixed vegetables, if you like.

JERK CHICKEN

Even though there are obligatory ingredients that go into jerk, recipes vary wildly from person to person. Dry rub or wet marinade (or both)? Vinegar or lime juice? Pimento (allspice) on its own or boosted with other spices?

This is my recipe. It was conceived in Jamaica but very much born in the UK. I don't use pimento wood—which is abundant on the island—to cook mine, since I can't get hold of it easily, it's too expensive, and using it in London is unsustainable. Plus I like using bay to smoke. Bay trees are easier to find, and I've met so many people through putting shout-outs on social media asking if I can come and prune their tree! They're usually grateful for the free gardening… And using bay, I feel that my recipe reflects the environment in which it is eaten and enjoyed, while still remaining true to the original. When bay is used with soaked pimento (allspice) berries and a bit of applewood, it gives a flavor close to pimento smoke (though you can simply use applewood chips and pimento berries if you can't find bay either).

Jerk takes time. It's important to layer the flavors. I start with a wet marinade, which is left to infuse for at least 24 hours and ideally 48.

Then, when it's time to cook, ideally you'll do so over coals on the grill. I light a fire and, once it's died down, layer the bay on top and place the chicken directly on the branches and leaves. Then I throw some soaked pimento (allspice) berries on and cook the chicken slowly. It's stunning.

A lot of people will say that, without smoke, it's not jerk. And while that's true, it's not to say you can't enjoy the flavors of jerk if you don't have access to a barbecue or outside space. It can be cooked in the oven. It won't be the same, but it'll still be delicious.

Ingredient note
When using pimento (allspice), first smell it. Some pimento will have only a faint smell and, if so, I recommend adding 1 tsp each of ground cinnamon and ground cloves to the marinade mixture, as well as ½ tsp grated nutmeg. If the pimento is fragrant and already smells of cloves, nutmeg, and even vanilla, you don't have to add the other ingredients.

8 chicken legs, skin on

For the marinade
2 oz (60 g) piece of ginger, roughly chopped
4 scallions, roughly chopped
1 small onion, roughly chopped
2 tbsp dried pimento (allspice) berries
2 tsp sea salt
2 tbsp sugar
6 garlic cloves, peeled
15 thyme sprigs, roughly stripped
 (just remove the largest twigs)
4 tbsp apple cider vinegar
1 tbsp black peppercorns
1 Scotch bonnet, deseeded or not depending
 on heat tolerance

To grill (optional)
a lot of bay branches and leaves
handful of applewood chips
handful of dried pimento (allspice) berries

To serve (optional)
plantain, Rice & Peas, Roasted Breadfruit,
 Fried Dumpling, Apple Coleslaw, Pepper
 Sauce Mayo, and Jerk Chicken Gravy (see
 pages 231, 219, 224, 126, 47, and 139)

Stab the chicken legs with your knife about 6 times, all over, to create pockets into which you can push marinade.

Put the marinade ingredients in a food processor and blend to a fine paste. Pour the paste over the legs and rub it in all over, including in all the slashes so it penetrates the flesh. Cover and refrigerate for at least 24 hours, ideally 48 hours.

Return the chicken to room temperature.

If you are cooking on a lidded barbecue, gather bay branches and leaves and cut them to fit the size of your barbecue. Soak the handful of pimento berries and the handful of applewood chips in a bowl of water for at least 30 minutes.

Light the barbecue, and, once the coals are glowing white, spread them out. Don't start with too much charcoal or the grill will be too hot; you can add more coals on top of the smouldering ones during cooking if needed to maintain the temperature.

Cover the grill grate with the bay branches and leaves and lay the chicken on top. Drain the pimento berries and wood chips. Scatter some over the bay and the rest over the coals. Close the lid, closing the bottom vents to halfway while leaving the top vents fully open.

The chicken legs will take between 30 minutes and 1 hour to cook, depending on the grill temperature. If you've got a meat thermometer, stick it into the thickest part of the biggest leg and if it says 165°F (70°C), you're good. If not, keep cooking until it reaches the right temperature. If you don't have a thermometer, take a leg out after 40 minutes and insert a knife into the thickest part. If the juices run clear, it's cooked.

Push the bay aside and finish the chicken directly over the coals to fully brown the skin.

To cook in an oven, preheat the oven to 350°F (180°C). Place the chicken on a baking sheet and cook for 30 minutes. Check the legs are cooked, as above, then finish under a hot broiler for 6 minutes to brown the skin.

However you cooked it, remove from the heat, rest for 10 minutes, then portion the chicken with a chopper (cleaver).

Serve with any or all of plantain, Rice & Peas, or Roasted Breadfruit or Fried Dumpling, with Apple Coleslaw if you like, Pepper Sauce Mayo, and a jug of Jerk Chicken Gravy to drizzle all over.

Clockwise from top left: Pepper Sauce Mayo, Rice & Peas, Pepper Sauce, Roasted Breadfruit, Jerk Chicken, Apple Coleslaw, Fried Dumpling (center) (see pages 47, 231, 278, 219, 148, 126, and 224)

Meat

Cooking meat in Jamaica has historically been a lesson in patience, majoring as it does on tough cuts made tender and delicious through that most precious ingredient: time.

The island led the way in "fifth quarter" eating—those extremities and offal left behind once the prize cuts had been taken away—for centuries. That story is told in dishes such as stewed oxtail, which is only done when it's done and not a moment before.

Curry goat celebrates the island's unique makeup. A meat loved around the world, goat is now thankfully more accessible to people in countries that have missed out for so long. Online retail means you can easily get hold of it. The same applies to mutton, which I love for its rich flavor.

Pork is less popular in Jamaica these days, though historically it was a vital protein source, especially for the Maroons (see page 160), who laid the foundations for jerk when cooking the island's wild pigs. And the jerk pits of Boston still prize pigs; some even have slaughterhouses out back to dispatch the animals before they hit the pimento wood grills.

JERK PORK

Jerk pork is where it all began in the 17th century and, although this dish has evolved, it always feels special to make it. At the jerk pits in Boston, pork is one of the best-sellers. Some pits have slaughterhouses out back where they slaughter the pigs in preparation for a long, slow roast over pimento wood. It is unbeatable with sides of Pressed Plantain, Roasted Breadfruit, Apple Coleslaw, and Pepper Sauce (see pages 215, 219, 126, and 278) and a bottle of chilled Red Stripe beer. I urge you to make it, close your eyes, and imagine yourself in the heady heat of the Jamaican sun.

To speed up the cooking time, ask your butcher to slice the belly into strips; in fact, jerk pork is quite often sold as slices. Cook slices as instructed for 1–1½ hours until the meat pulls apart with a bit of pressure, and then finish directly over the coals to get a nice char. Leave to rest for 10 minutes, then serve.

If you don't have a barbecue, you can still make this. Place in an oven preheated to 400°F (200°C) before reducing the temperature to 285°F (140°C). Cook for 4 hours, remove and rest, then serve.

SERVES 6

3 lb 5 oz (1.5 kg) piece of pork belly, with skin and bone

For the marinade
2 oz (60 g) piece of ginger, roughly chopped
4 scallions, roughly chopped
3 tbsp dried pimento (allspice) berries
1½ tbsp sugar
1 garlic bulb, cloves separated and peeled
20 thyme sprigs, roughly stripped
4 tbsp white wine vinegar, or apple cider vinegar
1–2 Scotch bonnets, to taste, deseeded or not depending on heat tolerance
2 tsp sea salt
2 tbsp freshly ground black pepper

To grill
a lot of bay branches and leaves (or just use applewood chips)
cupful of dried pimento (allspice) berries
handful of applewood chips

To serve
Jerk Chicken Gravy, Pressed Plantain, Roasted Breadfruit, Apple Coleslaw, and Pepper Sauce (see pages 139, 215, 219, 126, and 278)

Blend all the marinade ingredients in a food processor or blender until smooth.

Take the pork and poke it all over with the point of a sharp knife. Put it in a roasting pan deeper than the belly and rub the marinade all over, poking it into the slashes made by the knife. Leave to marinate in the fridge for at least 24 hours and up to 36.

Remove the pork belly from the fridge 2 hours before cooking.

Gather bay branches and leaves and cut them to fit the size of your grill. Soak the pimento berries and wood chips in a bowl of water for at least 30 minutes.

Prepare a lidded barbecue for indirect cooking, with the coals pushed to one side. Light it and wait for the fire to burn down and the coals to be glowing. Place the bay branches over the side away from the coals and place the pork belly on top of them. Drain the pimento berries and wood chips. Scatter some over the bay and the rest over the coals.

Close the lid of the barbecue, closing the bottom vents to two-thirds shut, aiming for a temperature of 265–300°F (130–150°C). Fully open the top vents.

Cook for 3–4 hours, or until the pork yields under minimum pressure from a finger or a chopstick. You may have to top up the coals to maintain the heat throughout cooking.

Remove the pork belly, wrap in parchment paper, and rest for at least 30 minutes. Slice and serve with Jerk Chicken Gravy alongside Pressed Plantain, Roasted Breadfruit, Apple Coleslaw, and Pepper Sauce.

BREAKFAST & LUNCH
JERK PORK·JERK CHICKEN
FISH:STEAM·ROAST FRY
SHRIMP:CURRY ,GARLIC
ROAST SWEET POTATO·ROAST YAM
BREADFRUIT· FESTIVAL·RICE & PEAS

A jerk shack in Boston

Jerk

"We had at dinner... a barbecued pig, the best and richest dishes that I ever tasted; the latter, in particular which was dressed in the true Maroon fashion, being placed on a barbecue (a frame of wicker-work, through whose interstices the steam can ascend), filled with peppers and spices of the highest flavor, wrapt in plantain leaves, and then buried in a hole filled with hot stones, by whose vapour it is baked, no particle of the juice being thus suffered to evaporate. I have eaten several other good Jamaica dishes, but none so excellent as this."
Matthew Gregory Lewis, *Journal of a West India Proprietor*, 1834

Ask a non-Jamaican to name a Jamaican dish and chances are that they will say jerk. Little wonder, because few Jamaican dishes capture the imagination quite like it.

Good jerk is incredible: smoky, full of flavor, texturally perfect. It is a celebration, a statement, it takes time and it takes care. The evolution of this wondrous dish came about through a specific set of circumstances and the input of various early settlers.

Fire-cooking in Jamaica goes back to at least the Taíno (see page 34), indeed, the Arawak word *barbacoa* gave us the word barbecue. The Taíno were expert in the art of barbecue cooking. They devised a wooden frame to hold the fish—the main protein eaten by the Taíno—to be cooked. This was then placed over the fire and they could adjust its height: low so the meat or fish cooked quickly, or high to smoke and preserve it.

> "They roast the flesh on sticks which they place in the ground, like a grating or trivet, over a pit, they call these barbacoas, and place fire beneath, and in this manner they roast fish also. Since the land is naturally hot, even though it is tempered by Divine Providence, fish and meat soon spoil if they are not roasted on the same day they are killed or caught." Gonzalo Fernández de Oviedo y Valdés, *Natural History of the West Indies*, 1525

When the Spanish colonizers landed, they brought pigs to Jamaica and, inevitably, some of the animals escaped to roam wild.

Subsequently, when England captured Jamaica in 1655, many of the enslaved people either fled or were freed. They escaped to the remotest parts of the island, often to the mountains, where they joined other Africans who had escaped Spanish slavery, who were known as "Maroons." (The name is thought to derive from the Spanish *cimarrón*, meaning "wild" or "untamed" and used specifically to describe runaways.) They also formed vital connections with the few remaining Taíno. It is believed some intermarried, continuing the Amerindian line; certainly Maroon communities are still very much present in Jamaica today and are proud of their ancestry.

The Maroons built communities in the isolated mountainous areas where they lived on the land; cultivating food and using herbs and plants for remedies, many of which are still used today in Maroon communities and beyond. They also hunted wild pigs and deer for food. A kill ensured food, and preservation of the meat guaranteed sustenance during lean hunting or foraging times. Jerk as we know it today could have evolved from this early method of preserving meat using the island's spices.

As the British built Jamaica into a slave society, however, hostilities between the two groups grew. The British attempted to recapture the freed Maroons, who in turn defended their territory. This led to what has been described as

a guerrilla war against the British, with Maroons carrying out raids on the British camps. The British thirst for domination meant the Maroons' freedom posed a problem; it threatened the smooth running of the British slave society and it blocked their expansion to certain parts of the island. It also made potential British settlers reluctant to come to Jamaica.

To avoid detection by the British, the Taíno taught the Maroons how to cook in covered pits, so as to create as little tell-tale smoke as possible. They also showed them how to preserve meat: they cut an animal open, salted it, and left it in the sun to cure—which the Maroons called *jirking* the meat—before placing it in the fire pit. Hans Sloane described the process of "jirking" pigs:

> "… They are shot or pierc'd through with Lances, cut open, the Bones taken out, and the Flesh is gash'd on the inside into the skin, fill'd with Salt and expos'd to the Sun, which is call'd Jirking. It is so brought home to their Masters by the Hunters, and eats much as Bacon, if broil'd on Coals."

Together, the Maroons and their Taíno cooking teachers used basic spicing to aid the preservation process, as much as for the taste. They used bird pepper and pimento (allspice)—the latter named by the Spanish colonizers who mistook it for black pepper—to spice the meat and then wrapped it in fragranced leaves, usually pepper elder, a beautifully aromatic plant, although there are also records of plantain leaves being used. And thus jerk was born, albeit an early version of the dish.

But where the name "jerk" originated remains debatable. Some believe it is derived from an indigenous Peruvian food called *charqui*, strips of dried meat similar to jerky. Others claim it comes from the process of "jerking" the meat, in other words poking holes in an animal so that spices could permeate the flesh before cooking.

Between 1739 and 1740, the Leeward and Windward Maroons signed a treaty with the British government, signing over tracts of lands to them. In return, the Maroons agreed to hand over enslaved Africans who had run away from British plantations. Although some Maroon communities accused their leaders of selling out over the treaty, others questioned just how strictly that part of the deal was enforced anyway. But the treaty undoubtedly afforded the Maroons relative freedom and meant that they could become more enterprising with their jerk.

"In the days of slavery, the Maroon huntsman was a fine specimen of the athletic negro, on whom was stamped the impress of the Freeman. He was generally seen in the towns armed with a fowling piece and cutlass, and belts that suspended on one side a large plaited bag, known as a 'cuttacoo,' and on the other a calabash, guarded with a netted covering, in which he carried his supply of water. On his back, braced round his shoulders, and suspended by a bandage over the forehead, was generally seen the wicker cradle, that held inclosed a side of jerked hog, which he sold passing along, in measured slices, to ready customers, as an especial delicacy for the breakfast table."

Phillip Henry Gosse, *A Naturalist's Sojourn in Jamaica*, 1851

Thus, gradually, this way of preserving and cooking pork wound its way down the mountains and into people's homes across Jamaica.

Today, jerk is everywhere in Jamaica, and anywhere there is a Jamaican diaspora, including the UK and US. Many families have their own prized recipes, while commercially produced sauces are there for those who don't. But as its popularity has increased, so have the poor imitations. Be they fast food stores serving jerk burgers, supermarkets selling jerk wraps, or celebrity chefs making "jerk" that just isn't jerk, they have little connection to the true dish.

It's a bugbear of mine.

A dish with such an illustrious history, which survived in the unlikeliest of circumstances to become known around the world, is precious. But that's not to say that I frown upon all change. In Jamaica, the impracticality of a jerk pit has given way to the ubiquitous oil-drum and gas-canister jerk pans, seen everywhere on the island. Jamaicans use a lot of imported gas and oil, and, once the contents of the drums and canisters are spent, they are often discarded on the side of the road. Now, they have a purpose. I even found out recently that down the road from me in South East London, someone turns old oil drums into jerk pans.

So, obviously, I got one.

CRISPY GINGER BEER PORK BELLY

This dish is a real mix of influences. It started as a recipe at my pop-up dinners, where I cooked Japanese-inspired comfort food, and was based on a Japanese braised pork dish. But I preferred my pork to have some bite, some crisp. So I would braise it in a liquid that eventually incorporated Jamaican ginger beer, then chill it and slice it.

Now it has evolved into a preparation similar to *siu yuk*, Chinese crispy roast pork. It feels fitting with the Chinese influence in Jamaica, plus the pigs that ran wild in the mountains and sustained Maroon communities there. It's a beautiful fusion dish, works brilliantly, and gives fail-safe crispy crackling every single time.

SERVES 6-8

4½ lb (2 kg) piece of boneless pork belly, with skin
6 scallions, cut into 1 in (3 cm) pieces
3 in (7.5 cm) piece of ginger, finely sliced
6 garlic cloves, peeled
1 tbsp black peppercorns
2 tsp dried pimento (allspice) berries
2 tsp tamarind extract
3 tbsp (30 g) sea salt flakes, plus 1 tsp
2 × 11 oz (330 ml) cans of Old Jamaica Ginger Beer (not diet)
1-2 tbsp apple cider vinegar, plus more to rub the skin

To serve (all optional)
rice, salad, and greens

Slice the rind of the pork at ¾ in (2 cm) intervals, being careful not to cut as deep as the flesh (or ask your butcher to do this). Preheat the oven to 400°F (200°C).

Put the scallions, ginger, garlic, peppercorns, pimento, half the tamarind extract, and 1 teaspoon of salt in a baking dish that can comfortably hold the pork, as well as being deeper than it. Pour over the ginger beer, then place the pork on top.

Cover, seal with foil, and roast for 20 minutes. Reduce the oven temperature to 265°F (130°C) and cook for another 2½ hours. Leave the pork in the oven until it's cool enough to handle. Remove and carefully lift the pork out and onto a flat plate. Strain the liquid through a sieve and reserve it; discard the aromatics.

Once the pork is cool, preheat the oven to 320°F (160°C). Wipe the rind with a piece of paper towel splashed with a little vinegar and then carefully spread the 1 oz (30 g) of sea salt on top of the skin, ensuring as much is covered as possible. The surface will be uneven but the salt should still stick, mostly.

Return the pork to the oven for 30 minutes, then remove it. Increase the oven temperature to 440°F (225°C). The salt should have formed a crust which will be easy to remove, just brush off any remaining bits now. Return the pork to the oven for 20-35 minutes until the skin has puffed up and is crispy.

Meanwhile, take the reserved cooking liquid and heat it in a saucepan over medium heat. Add the 1-2 tablespoons of vinegar, to taste, and the remaining 1 teaspoon tamarind extract. Cook until it is dark and glossy, but keep an eye on it as it can easily reduce too much and become too sticky to use.

Turn the pork belly onto its crispy skin and cut into strips—using the slashes on the skin as guides—then cut those into ¾ in (2 cm) chunks.

Pour the cooking liquid over the meat—avoiding the skin—and serve with rice, salad, and greens such as callaloo, spinach, or kale, if you like.

STEWED OXTAIL

Cattle became plentiful in the Greater Antilles after they were brought over by the Spanish from Columbus's second voyage in 1493. A single Spaniard was said to have owned 40,000 cattle alone. In Jamaica, many of them became wild towards the end of Spain's tenure and were then rounded up into pens by the English.

Enslaved people were given provision grounds to grow vegetables, and rations of meat or fish. But it was rarely the prime cuts, which the white slavers would keep. The meat-to-bone ratio of oxtail, together with its long cooking time, meant it was particularly unfavored. This dish is evidence of the resourcefulness of the African population. Given time, and flavor, it is a luxurious, melt-in-the-mouth delicacy, as evidenced now by its astronomical price.

If there are any leftovers—and I've devised this recipe so that there might be—I urge you to make Oxtail Nuggets (see page 47). They're a delight.

SERVES 4

3 lb 5 oz (1.5 kg) oxtail (most come already jointed but, if not, ask your butcher to do it)
white wine vinegar or apple cider vinegar
1 tsp sea salt
2 tsp freshly ground black pepper
1½ tbsp ground pimento (allspice)
2 tsp onion powder
2 tsp garlic powder
1 tbsp all-purpose seasoning
1 tbsp Savory Browning (optional, see page 275)
3 onions, chopped
4 scallions, chopped
4 garlic cloves, very finely chopped
3 in (7.5 cm) piece of ginger, finely chopped
6 thyme sprigs
1 Scotch bonnet
1⅔ cups (400 ml) water
1 tbsp tomato paste
1 tbsp soy sauce
1 tbsp tamarind extract or Worcestershire sauce (optional)
2 carrots, chopped into rounds
14 oz (400 g) can of butter beans, drained

To serve
rice or Roasted Breadfruit (see page 219)

Wash the oxtail in a bowl of cold water and vinegar (see page 288). Drain well. Pat the meat dry and place in a clean, dry bowl.

Season the oxtail with the salt, pepper, pimento, onion powder, garlic powder, all-purpose seasoning, and Browning, if using.

Heat a Dutch pot or heavy-based pot over medium-high heat and brown the oxtail all over, starting with the fatty sides to render the fat so you don't need to add any oil. Brown for 10–15 minutes, until it's dark caramelized all over. Don't worry if the bottom of the pot has lots of seasoning stuck to it; it's all part of the flavor.

Add the onions, scallions, garlic, ginger, thyme, and Scotch bonnet to the pot (keeping it whole for flavor or finely chop ¼–½ for heat), continuously stirring so they don't catch. Cook for 10 minutes, until the onions are softened and starting to brown. If you kept the Scotch bonnet whole, you can remove it at any point, depending on how hot you'd like the finished dish to be.

Pour in the measured water, tomato paste, soy sauce, and tamarind extract. Bring to a boil, then reduce the heat to low, cover with a lid, and cook for 2–3½ hours, until the meat is coming off the bone and the fat has risen. The time this takes will depend on the meat and cooking conditions. Once it's ready, add the carrots and butter beans and cook for a further 20 minutes, without the lid, until the carrots are soft.

Turn the heat off and leave to settle, then skim off as much of the fat as possible. Pick out the thyme sprigs if you want and the whole Scotch bonnet, if using. If eating the following day, chill it and the fat will be easier to remove.

Serve with rice or Roasted Breadfruit.

CURRY GOAT

Spend any time in Jamaica and eventually you'll see goats wandering around the streets, inquisitively sticking their noses everywhere. They arrived here with the Spanish, became wild once they left, and were used as livestock. But they really hit Jamaica's culinary walk of fame with the introduction of indentured servants from India, brought in after the abolition of slavery to make up the labor shortfall.

Now curry goat is a signature Jamaican dish, known throughout the world and still enjoyed on the island. It was one of the first dishes I ever made for friends. I love the whole process: getting the meat from the butcher and watching them cut it with a bandsaw, then bringing it home to cook slowly. I have many happy memories associated with it; I hope you will cook this and make it your own.

SERVES 4-6

3 lb 5 oz (1.5 kg) goat meat on the bone,
   cut in chunks by your butcher
a little white wine vinegar, or apple
   cider vinegar
3 garlic cloves, very finely chopped
2 onions, chopped
3 tbsp Jamaican curry powder
   (for homemade, see page 23)
1 tbsp all-purpose seasoning
1 tsp sea salt
1 tsp freshly ground black pepper
3 tbsp vegetable oil, plus more if needed
3 thyme sprigs
1 tsp ground pimento (allspice)
1⅔ cups (400 ml) water
1 Scotch bonnet
2 potatoes, peeled, then cut into
   1 in (3 cm) pieces

To serve
Rice & Peas, Quick Roti, and Steamed
   Cabbage (see pages 231, 235, and 123)

Wash the goat meat in a bowl of water mixed with a little vinegar (see page 288). Rinse and drain well, then pat the meat dry.

In a clean, dry bowl, mix the goat meat with the garlic, onions, curry powder, all-purpose seasoning, salt, and pepper. Cover and leave for 2 hours in the fridge.

Heat the oil in a Dutch pot or a large, heavy pot over medium heat. Scrape all the marinade from the goat into a separate bowl and sear the goat meat all over in the oil; it should take around 10 minutes.

Add the marinade to the pot along with the thyme, pimento, and a bit more oil if needed. Cook until the onions start to soften. Pour in the measured water and bring to a boil, then reduce the heat to a simmer.

Pierce the Scotch bonnet with a knife, ensuring you don't cut it too much, then add it to the pot, stir it in, and cover with a lid. Once it's bubbling, reduce the heat to low and simmer for 1–1½ hours until the meat is tender and the fat has separated and risen to the top. Pick out the thyme sprigs along with the Scotch bonnet, if you want.

Add the potatoes and cook until they are tender, 10–15 minutes.

Serve with Rice & Peas, Quick Roti, and Steamed Cabbage.

TAMARIND & GINGER ROAST LAMB

Tamarind is abundant in Jamaica and, happily, it goes with nearly everything. Here, its tanginess excites the lamb. This is a deliciously sticky dish that is perfect for a lazy Sunday. We cook it so there's still a bit of bite to the meat, but if you would rather it was pull-apart tender, then cover it in foil for the first two hours of cooking and then remove the cover for the rest.

SERVES 6-8

14 oz (400 g) tamarind pods, or 2 tbsp
   tamarind extract
1 in (2.5 cm) piece of ginger, chopped
4 garlic cloves
1 tbsp ground ginger
1 tsp ground pimento (allspice)
leaves from 4 thyme sprigs
½ tsp ground cinnamon
1 tsp ground cumin
2 scallions, sliced
2 tsp sea salt
1 lamb shoulder on the bone (3⅓-4½ lb/
   1.5-2 kg)
2 onions, sliced

To serve
roasted yam and Steamed Cabbage
   (see page 123)

If using tamarind pods, remove the flesh, pit them, and pick off any strings. Bring to a boil in a saucepan with a scant 1 cup (200 ml) water, then reduce to a simmer, stirring constantly, until thick. It will take around 12 minutes.

In a food processor, blend all the ingredients apart from the lamb and sliced onions—but including the tamarind—until they form a paste. Rub the paste all over the lamb, pushing it into any nooks and crannies. Leave to marinate for 4 hours or overnight in the fridge.

Remove from the fridge 1 hour before cooking, so the meat can return to room temperature. Preheat the oven to 400°F (200°C).

Scatter the sliced onions into a roasting pan, add a cupful of water, and sit the lamb on top. Place the lamb in the oven and immediately reduce the oven temperature to 300°F (150°C). Cook for 3 hours.

Remove the lamb from the oven, cover loosely with foil, and let rest for 20 minutes.

Serve with roasted yam and Steamed Cabbage.

MUTTON HOTPOT

The origins of this dish lie not in Jamaica but in. . . *Coronation Street*, the beloved British soap opera. Betty worked at the Rover's Return pub in the long-running soap, and served hotpot to her customers. It's a dish popular in the North of England, especially Lancashire (though the show is based in a fictional Manchester satellite town) and I was obsessed with it. I didn't make it until I was in my thirties, and then I wondered if I could give it a Jamaican makeover. I replaced the potato with sweet potato, swapped lamb for mutton, and added some yam in there too. The result is a beautifully comforting dish. I love how the sweetness of the potato takes on the earthy flavor of the mutton, which is meltingly soft. It looks great too.

SERVES 6

1 sweet potato, peeled and finely sliced
1 lb (500 g) boneless mutton, in chunks
2 tbsp cornstarch
1½ tsp sea salt
1 tsp freshly ground black pepper
2 tbsp vegetable oil
2 onions, chopped
3 garlic cloves, very finely chopped
3 thyme sprigs
2 cups (500 ml) stock (vegetable, chicken, or lamb, for homemade, see pages 127 and 138)
14 oz (400 g) white yam, peeled and chopped
2-3 carrots (about 10½ oz /300 g), chopped into ¾ in (2 cm) chunks
3½ tbsp (50 g) salted butter, melted

Bring a pot of water to a boil, drop in the sweet potato slices, and blanch for 8 minutes until softened. Drain.

Put the mutton in a large bowl and sprinkle with the cornstarch, salt, and pepper, tossing to coat.

Heat the oil in a heavy-based pot over medium heat and add the mutton. Brown the meat all over, cooking for 10 minutes. Add the onions, garlic, and thyme and fry for 10 minutes until the onions start to brown.

Pour in the stock and bring to a boil, then reduce the heat and simmer for 30 minutes. Add the yam and carrots and cook for another 5 minutes.

Meanwhile, preheat the oven to 350°F (180°C).

Transfer the hotpot to a baking dish (round if you have one), picking out the thyme sprigs if you want, then lay the sweet potato slices on top in a spiral, starting from the outside and finishing in the center.

Brush with the melted butter and cook in the oven for 45–50 minutes. Remove, let it rest for 10 minutes, then serve.

MUTTON CHOPS WITH EGGPLANT & TOMATO

This is a dish I've honed for years and it never lets me down.

"Mutton" and "goat" are terms that can often be used interchangeably in Jamaica and elsewhere, but this dish uses mutton chops from sheep; the maturity of the mutton makes them particularly lovely.

This recipe has elements of Jamaica's famous curry mutton in its use of spices, but the chops here are grilled quickly rather than slow cooked as they would be for curry. Once the fat gets going, the taste is sensational. The accompanying salad is something we had growing up and everything together is just such a beautiful combination. I love it.

SERVES 4

1 tbsp ground cumin
1 tbsp ground coriander
1 tsp ground turmeric
2 tsp freshly ground black pepper
1 tbsp Thyme Salt (see page 119)
8 mutton chops
4 garlic cloves, very finely chopped
   or finely grated
4 tbsp plain yogurt
handful of parsley leaves, finely chopped
a little vegetable oil (optional)

For the salad
2 eggplants
1½ tbsp apple cider vinegar
1½ tbsp olive oil
½ red onion, finely sliced
2 large tomatoes, 5½–6½ oz (160–180g each),
   roughly chopped
sea salt

Mix the spices and Thyme Salt together and rub well into the mutton chops. Add 3 of the garlic cloves, rub in, and leave while you prepare the eggplant salad.

Slice the eggplants into ⅛ in (3 mm) slices and cook on your grill or a grill pan over medium heat without oil for 5–7 minutes per side until the slices are cooked through; you can tell by the change in texture. Continue until all the eggplants are cooked, then cut each slice into halves or quarters, depending on size.

In a small bowl, mix together the vinegar, olive oil, and red onion and season well, then mix this dressing with the eggplants and add the tomatoes. Set aside.

Mix the yogurt with the remaining garlic, the parsley, and a pinch of salt.

If you are cooking on a lidded barbecue, set it up for indirect cooking—with coals set to one side—and light it. If you are using a grill pan and oven, preheat the oven to 350°F (180°C).

If using a barbecue, place the chops away from the coals, close the lid, and cook for 15 minutes until brown. Transfer the chops to sit directly over the coals. Keep turning until they get a good crust, not neglecting the fat edge, as you want that to sizzle too. Keep turning and cooking for 5–10 minutes until they are a lovely brown all over.

If cooking indoors, rub some vegetable oil over the chops and place, fat edges down, on a hot grill pan. Cook for 2–3 minutes until the fat starts to render, then move the chops on to one side, and cook for another 3–4 minutes until they begin to take on some color. Flip the chops and repeat on the other side before placing on a baking pan and cooking in the oven for 8–10 minutes, depending on their thickness and how well cooked you would like them.

However you have cooked the chops, rest them for 5 minutes. Serve with the eggplant and tomatoes and the yogurt sauce on the side.

PEPPER GOAT SKEWERS

While much of the world loves goat meat and has taken it to its heart, the UK and US have lagged behind. Brits and Americans drink goat milk and eat goat cheese, but the majority don't yet seem to have made the connection to male kid dairy goats that are killed at birth because there isn't a big enough market for their meat.

As someone who has grown up eating goat, this seems like a massive shame. And gradually more people are getting clued up about it, thanks to people like Nadia and Nick Stokes, who used to run a Cypriot restaurant built around goat meat, and James Whetlor who runs Cabrito, a company that sells goat meat online.

Unlike curry goat, which calls for an older animal that can take a long cook, this recipe calls for kid goat meat: younger and more tender, thus requiring less cooking. So skewers are perfect.

MAKES 8-10, SERVES 4-6

1 lb (500 g) kid goat meat, cut into
   1 in (3 cm) chunks
1-3 Scotch bonnets, finely chopped,
   to taste, deseeded or not depending
   on heat tolerance
3 garlic cloves, crushed
½ onion, finely chopped
½ tsp ground pimento (allspice)
½ tsp freshly ground black pepper
2 tsp onion powder
2 tsp garlic powder
1 tsp dried thyme
½ tsp ground turmeric
1 tsp ground cumin
2 tsp smoked paprika
1 tsp sea salt
1 tbsp oil, plus more for cooking
lime wedges and undressed ("naked")
   coleslaw (optional), to serve

Marinate the goat in all the ingredients, including the 1 tablespoon oil, but not the oil for cooking, for at least 4 hours in the fridge. Make sure to return the meat to room temperature before cooking.

Heat 2 frying pans, one dry and the other containing 2 tablespoons of oil.

Scrape the marinade off the goat into a separate bowl and skewer the meat, using 4-6 pieces on each skewer, depending on their length.

Cook the marinade in the frying pan with the oil for 10 minutes until the onion is soft and starting to caramelize.

Rub more oil over the goat skewers and fry in the dry frying pan for 8 minutes, turning to brown on all sides.

Spoon the onion mixture on to a serving plate, keeping a little back. Lay the skewers on top and scatter the reserved onion mixture over them. Serve with lime wedges and accompany with "naked" coleslaw, if you like.

COFFEE RUBBED STEAK

Coffee is a brilliant ingredient in loads of different foods; it can add richness to a stew or lift a chocolate recipe. Here, it gives steak a really tasty savoriness, enhancing the meat's flavor. There is perhaps a slight bitterness from the coffee too, which is mellowed by the buttery flavor of the beef. I've seen a few people in the US make this dish, and as soon as I saw it, I had to give it a try. My version has pimento (allspice) and thyme, which are incredible with the coffee.

I'd recommend using the best beef you can afford, dry-aged if possible, with lovely yellow fat. And the best version of this recipe is made with Blue Mountain coffee brought back from Jamaica.

If you're cooking a bone-in steak, you may need to finish it off in an oven preheated to 350°F (180°C).

SERVES 2–3

1 tsp freshly ground black pepper
2 tsp ground pimento (allspice)
2 tsp Thyme Salt (see page 119)
2 tsp ground Blue Mountain coffee
1 × 1¾–2¼ lb (800 g–1 kg) bone-in steak
    (rib-eye, sirloin, T-bone. or tomahawk)
a little vegetable oil
3½ tbsp (50 g) salted butter
3 garlic cloves, crushed in their skins
leaves from 4 thyme sprigs

To serve
Cassava Fries and Pepper Sauce Mayo
    (see pages 220 and 47)

Mix the pepper, pimento, Thyme Salt, and coffee. Lay the steak on a plate and evenly coat it in the coffee mixture, including the edges, patting the mixture into the steak. Transfer to the fridge, uncovered, and leave for at least 8 hours and up to 36 hours.

Remove the steak from the fridge at least 45 minutes before cooking, so it gets up to room temperature. Rub it with a thin layer of oil.

Whether cooking inside or out, you need a grill pan or cast-iron pan suitable for your chosen cooking method, as well as a meat thermometer.

If cooking indoors, heat a heavy-based frying pan over medium-high heat.

If using a barbecue, light the coals in the middle of the grate and wait for it to heat up. Put your chosen pan on the grill to come to a good hot temperature.

Using a pair of tongs, hold the steak on the pan fat side down until the fat starts to color and render. Angle it to color as much of the surface as you can.

Now lay the steak down on one side and cook for 2 minutes. Using the tongs, move the steak around to ensure the color catches across the surface and then turn and brown the other side for 1–2 minutes. Drop in the butter, garlic, and thyme and baste the steak, holding the pan at an angle and using a spoon to scoop up the melted butter and pour it over the surface. Repeat 10 times.

Place a meat thermometer into the steak and remove it once it reaches your preference: 122–125°F (50–52°C) will be rare, 130–135°F (55–57°C) is medium-rare, and 140°F (60°C) is medium; the temperature will continue to rise as it rests. Place on a plate or baking pan with a lip that will catch the juices and rest for 8 minutes.

Once ready, slice and serve with Cassava Fries, Pepper Sauce Mayo, and a salad, if you like, pouring the buttery cooking juices over the steak.

MAUREEN'S COW FOOT

Maureen Tyne (see her right and overleaf) cooks some of the best food I've ever tasted. She grew up in St. Thomas, Jamaica, where she was taught to cook by her grandmother. She came over to the UK in the 1990s, settling in London. She'd cook for friends, who then asked her to cater for events, and her business grew by word of mouth.

She operates out of her home down Railton Road towards Herne Hill in South London. Because she doesn't use social media or a website, you wouldn't hear about it unless you were told about it. Or, if you're nosy like me, unless you'd noticed a backyard full of jerk pans and coal burners and then been invited to come in and have something to eat.

Maureen is brilliant: warm, funny, and an exciting chef. She serves jerk chicken, oxtail, curry goat, curry chicken, and fry chicken, and then on the weekend there's jerk pork, fry fish, mannish water, and cow foot.

Cow foot isn't a dish I grew up eating, but I love it and really wanted to include a recipe here. So Maureen shared hers with me. If you're ever in South London, find her. Just look for the jerk pans.

SERVES 4–6

1 cow foot (about 14 oz/400 g), cleaned and
   cut into 2 in (5 cm) pieces by your butcher
a little white wine vinegar or apple
   cider vinegar
2 scallions, chopped
1 onion, finely chopped
½ red bell pepper, finely chopped
1 tsp ground pimento (allspice)
3 garlic cloves, crushed
1 tsp freshly ground black pepper
2 tbsp all-purpose seasoning
¼ tsp paprika
¼ tsp turmeric
1 tbsp Savory Browning (see page 275)
vegetable oil
2½ cups (600 ml) water
2 × 14 oz (400 g) cans of butter beans,
   drained

To serve
plain rice or Rice & Peas (optional,
   see page 231)

Wash the cow foot in water and vinegar (see page 288). Put it in a bowl with all the other ingredients except the oil, measured water, and butter beans. Cover and leave to marinate for a minimum of 2 hours in the fridge.

In a heavy pot, heat a little oil over medium heat. Pick the cow foot out of its marinade and brown it all over. Add the rest of the marinade ingredients and brown those as well, before adding the measured water. Bring to a boil, then reduce the heat to a simmer and cook until the cow foot is tender to the touch, 2–3 hours.

Add the butter beans, cook for another 10 minutes, then serve with plain rice or Rice & Peas.

Grits, Grains & Hard Food

The starchy foods that grow in Jamaica give rise to an abundance of recipes and inspiration. Along with dumplings, they are collectively known as "hard food." Often, they are just boiled and served alongside a main dish; that simplicity allowing all the flavors and textures to shine in a way that is pure comfort.

Other starches need more preparation. Cassava makes the best fries; once they have been boiled to frilly perfection and then fried, the crisp is unreal. And I could write a book on plantain alone. I can't even walk past a pile of them without stopping to pick some up, even though I know I've got some at home.

Wheat and rice were first brought to Mexico by the Spanish in the 16th century; wheat was sown on the US mainland at the start of the 17th century and only once it established was it traded with the Caribbean. Nowadays, it features in so many of Jamaica's bakes, while rice and peas is world famous.

And if you're unfamiliar with Jamaican cooking, you might wonder: why so many types of dumpling? Because you can never have enough dumpling, that's why.

Evan, bammy maker, checking a bammy is cooked through in Pepper, St. Elizabeth

CORNMEAL PORRIDGE

Porridge is a hugely popular breakfast dish in Jamaica, made from lots of different starchy foods from peanuts to plantain. Cornmeal was popularized in the Caribbean with the movement of indigenous people from the American mainland—where they used corn to a greater extent—to the islands. Some believe that the tradition of eating porridge is a combination of Scottish and West African influences. Before turning to stolen labor from Africa, Scots, along with the Irish, Welsh, and English, operated on both sides of the trade; some were transported to the Caribbean as indentured servants or because they were convicts, while others were themselves enslavers.

However, writing in the 16th century, before the British arrived, Oviedo wrote of the island's colonizers: "The Christians pour [coconut milk] into the meal that they make of corn, making something like porridge."

It's not at all traditional, but I sometimes eat this porridge with Festival (see page 223).

SERVES 4-6

1¼ cups (200 g) fine cornmeal
1 cinnamon stick, or ½ tsp ground cinnamon
¼ tsp grated nutmeg
1⅔ cups (400 ml) water
scant 1 cup (200 ml) coconut milk
   (for homemade, see page 271)
scant 1 cup (200 ml) condensed milk
2 tbsp soft light brown sugar
1 tsp vanilla extract
sliced banana, to serve (optional)

Put the cornmeal, cinnamon, nutmeg, and measured water into a saucepan and stir to make sure it is fully incorporated.

Set over medium-low heat, stirring constantly for 5 minutes until it starts to thicken, then add the coconut milk, condensed milk, sugar, and vanilla extract.

Keep stirring for another 5 minutes, then serve. I like it with sliced banana.

MACARONI CHEESE

Whatever you call it—macaroni pie, mac 'n' cheese—few dishes ignite as much intense debate as this. There are so many different ways to make it... Saucy or dry? Which cheese? With eggs or not?

   A slice of macaroni cheese is a standard side dish in Jamaican takeout places and restaurants; it works really well with spicy dishes, as the creaminess calms the heat and makes it a perfect accompaniment. This is a slightly saucier version but, chilled, it slices well. Serve it alongside Thyme-Roasted Tomatoes (see page 119) for the ultimate flavor combination—the tomatoes' sweetness is incredible.

SERVES 6 AS A MAIN DISH, OR 8 AS A SIDE

5 tbsp (70 g) unsalted butter
generous ½ cup (70 g) all-purpose flour
2 tbsp oil (I use canola oil)
2 onions, sliced
scant 1 cup (200 ml) water
3⅓ cups (800 ml) whole milk
1 tsp mustard (I use English for extra punch)
1 tsp ground white pepper
1 tsp garlic powder
1¾ cups (200 g) Swiss cheese or Gouda, grated
1¾ cups (200 g) Cheddar cheese (I use mature), grated
1 cup (100 g) hard Italian cheese, such as Parmesan, finely grated
6½ cups (800 g) cooked macaroni (about 12 oz/350 g raw), cooked so it is still slightly hard (about 2 minutes less than the package suggests)

Heat the butter in a large pot and mix in the flour to make a paste (roux). Cook together for 10 minutes, stirring regularly.

Heat the oil in a separate pan and add the sliced onions. Pour in the measured water and cook over medium heat until the water evaporates and the onions become really soft. It'll take 12–15 minutes. Once ready, take off the heat.

Once the roux is ready, add the milk gradually, stirring constantly to incorporate as it goes in. It'll clump together at first, but eventually loosens up into a thick sauce.

Preheat the oven to 350°F (180°C).

Once all the milk has been stirred in, add the mustard, pepper, garlic powder, cooked onions, then the cheeses. Stir until the cheeses are melted and fully incorporated. Stir in the macaroni and mix well to try and get as much cheese into the middle of the pasta as you can.

Pour into a baking dish that can go under the broiler and bake for 10 minutes. Turn the broiler on, then cook under the heat for another 8 minutes until brown and bubbling.

Bammy in Pepper, St. Elizabeth, getting ready to be bagged up and taken to the market

BAMMY

Bammy are a labor of love, but totally worth it. The taste of them freshly cooked is so good, especially served with Fried Fish, so they get soaked in the escovitch sauce (see page 76). They are not cheap to buy ready-made, so I tend to make a big batch and freeze them.

I was lucky enough to watch bammy being made in Pepper, St. Elizabeth, by Evan and Patsy, who make hundreds every morning to sell at local markets. Watching the pair work, my mind immediately went to a description I'd read of Taíno preparing *casabe*, the flatbreads that are pretty identical to modern-day bammy (see page 201).

Ideally, you want bammy to remain white rather than brown, but, unless you're an expert—and I'm definitely not—it doesn't matter if you get a bit of color on them.

MAKES... IT DEPENDS!
A 2¼ LB (1 KG) CASSAVA YIELDS 8–10

1 cassava
sea salt

Peel the cassava thoroughly, removing any discolored bits, then chop into large chunks. Using a coarse grater, grate the chunks over a tray or large bowl, discarding the central fibrous core.

Squeeze the grated cassava between your hands. Place the squeezed cassava into a cheesecloth or tea towel in batches and squeeze as much liquid out as possible.

Weigh the dried-out cassava and add 1 teaspoon of sea salt for every 1 lb (500 g). Mix well.

Choose a pan to cook the bammy in with care, as its diameter will determine the size of the bammy. I use a 6 in (16 cm) diameter pan.

Put around 4 oz (120 g) of cassava meal in the pan. Press it down firmly using the base of a wide jar, or a flat press.

Cook over medium heat for 5–8 minutes or until cracks start to appear on the top and you can see the bammy has taken on a translucent appearance. Sprinkle some more cassava meal over the top, press down gently, then turn the bammy in the pan and press down again. Cook for another 5 minutes or until the bammy is totally translucent when held up to the light (see page 189). If there are any opaque patches, cook for longer until they disappear. At this point, bammy will keep for 2 days and can be frozen.

To serve the prepared bammy, soak them in water, milk, or coconut milk for 10 minutes, then fry in vegetable oil for 4 minutes until warmed through.

The view from my room at Tranquility Estate (see pages 111 and 227), of the foothills of the Blue Mountains

Jamaica's Larder

Sitting in the foothills of the Blue Mountains, I watch Jamaica slowly wake up as early morning fog rises above the beautiful vista; the sight takes my breath away. The mountains' edges are softened with a blanket of trees and big-leaved palms in every shade of green. Xaymaca has been claimed to mean "land of wood and water" in the Arawak language of the Taíno.

Look closer and details reveal themselves. Banana plants heavy with ripening fruit, their purple blossom hanging beneath. Unripe green mangos, soaking up the sun until they take on golden, rosy tones. I picture my dad as a boy, scrambling up the trunk to feast on their sweet orange flesh. Streams bustling with janga (crayfish or crawfish) if you know where to look. Cocoa pods with gnarled shiny skin ranging from yellow to red. Coconut palms. Trees bearing cloves, bay, pimento (allspice). Breadfruit and jackfruit, soursop, and pear.

I walk out past an ackee tree, its red fruit pods hanging from the branches, the ground below carpeted with the fallen black berries, as bountiful here on the island as apples are back in the British countryside. I get lost in a patch of sugar cane, my dad's childhood friend Winston cutting a cane for us to chew

199

on with one swipe of his machete. As I crunch its fibrous innards, the sweet juice floods my mouth. Chickens meander, pecking at the ground. Goats wander up the hillside, looking for their next snack. Roadside sellers offer piles of fruit and vegetables, from carrots to corn and cassava. Smoke rises as breadfruit roasts, its rough green skin turning black and ashy in the fire.

"You'll never go hungry here," says Christopher Binns. "Food is everywhere." Christopher is one half of Stush in the Bush, an incredible farmstead in St. Ann that is home to almost every conceivable edible plant in Jamaica, a concentration of everything found on the island. And his words are true. At its simplest, Jamaica's larder provides nourishment straight from the ground, tree, or bush. Food really is everywhere. And everything that grows here is so firmly ingrained in island culture, it's as though it has always been here. But it hasn't.

Like the island's people, much of the food here came from elsewhere, a consequence of myriad influences and migrations from across the world. These abundant ingredients are now the foundation for some of Jamaica's classic dishes: ackee and saltfish with a side of plantain, perhaps some boiled yam and green banana; soups filled with corn and carrots; bammy made from grated cassava, soaked in coconut milk and served with escovitch fried fish.

Jamaica's larder tells the story of the island's history in a meal, an ingredient, or just a piece of fruit.

What the First Settlers Ate

Although we know little about the lives of Jamaica's first-known inhabitants, save for the "Redware" pottery found during archaeological digs that gave them their modern-day name, the coastal location of two of their main settlements suggests fish was an important part of their diet. They also knew agriculture, a skill built upon by later Taíno who laid the foundation for some of the island food we know today. In the absence of written records, the little we know about what the Taíno of Jamaica grew and ate is gleaned through the records of the first Spanish colonizers to land in the Caribbean islands.

"They eat whenever they feel like it a little at a time, sitting on the ground, and they eat fish or meat in clay dishes," observed Bartolomé de las Casas in his *History of the Indies*.

Few quadrupeds existed in Jamaica until the Spaniards brought more livestock to the island, so the meat de las Casas describes could have been hutias, rodent-like animals native to Jamaica, which the Taíno captured and kept in pens to slaughter when needed. They also foraged for wild nuts and fruits.

Fish and seafood made up a lot of their protein consumption, and in Jamaica most Taíno villages were built in easy reach of the sea to enable a steady supply of lobster, conch, and shrimp—still enjoyed today—as well as turtles and iguana. Two large sea mammals—the manatee and monk seal—formed part of the diet too, the latter eventually becoming extinct.

Snapper, still the most common fish enjoyed in Jamaica, was eaten along with grouper, barracuda, and other creatures. They were caught using nets and spears, but also with a "sucker fish," which they kept in captivity. It would be released alongside a shoal of wild fish, and once it had latched on they'd use it to bring in the catch. Witnesses wrote of watching the Taíno fishermen give thanks to the fish.

Taíno society was agricultural and their conuco method of farming (see page 36) is still used in parts of Jamaica today. They grew sweet potatoes, squash, beans, peppers, and peanuts and "Indian corn"—maize—which was eaten raw when young, while older kernels were made into bread, which would have had to be consumed quickly because the humidity would turn it moldy.

Cassava (or manioc), known to the Taíno as yuca, was the most-prized crop. The Taíno are believed to have introduced cassava to the Caribbean, most likely transporting it with them on their migration from South America, and then cultivated it as a primary foodstuff. The cassava plant (*Manihot esculenta*) was so precious that their supreme deity (or zemi), Yucáhu, was named in its honor.

A bread they called *casabe* was made from the prolific cassava root. The cassava bread could last up to a year, which was a rare and vital benefit at a time when one ruined harvest could spell starvation. It also enabled the Taíno to take food with them while traveling.

Me with Lisa Binns at Stush in the Bush

One of the earliest known records of Taíno preparation of cassava was made by Gonzalo Fernández de Oviedo y Valdés—known as Oviedo—an early Spanish colonialist who journeyed to the Caribbean between 1514 and his death in 1557.

"In order to make bread of it, which is called cazabi (cassava), the Indians grate it and then press it in a strainer. . . The residue after the liquid is removed [is] cooked in the fire in a very hot flat clay vessel of the size they want the loaf to be. The mash is spread out, taking care that none of the liquid remains in it, then a loaf of the desired size is formed, which is necessarily the same size as the vessel in which it is baked. When the loaf has become firm it is removed from the fire and cured. Often, it is placed in the sun. The Indians then eat it for it is very good bread."

Laborious processing was needed to make cassava safe to eat, as, of the two types of cassava—bitter and sweet—the bitter contains potentially fatal levels of toxic chemicals. The Taíno passed this method of preparing cassava to the Spanish colonizers. It was still being practiced in the 17th century: in his *Voyage to the Islands* (1707), Hans Sloane described cassava being "bak'd as Oatcakes are in Scotland"... The bammy we enjoy today (see page 197) is a direct link to this bread and is prepared in an almost identical way. Soaked in coconut milk or water and then fried, it makes the perfect side to escovitch fried fish, escovitch itself being a remnant of Spanish immigration to the island. Escovitch comes from the Spanish *escabeche*, meaning to marinate in vinegar.

The Arrival of Spanish Imports

Although Spanish rule in Jamaica lasted just 146 years, its legacy is still felt in some dishes and ingredients they introduced. Columbus's second voyage to the Caribbean saw the introduction of many fruits, vegetables, and livestock to fuel a whole new Spanish colony. Peter Martyr wrote:

"Likewise mares, shiepe, heyghfers, and such other of bothe kindes for incrase. Lykewise all kynde of pulse or grayne and corne, as wheate, barlye, rye, beanes, and pease, and suche other, as well for food as to sowe: Belyde vynes, plantes and seedes, of suche trees, fruites, and herbes, as those countreyes lacke."

The Spaniards introduced much of the livestock that gave rise to classic Jamaican meat dishes, including cows, for oxtail and cow foot soup, goats for curry goat, and pigs that would run wild throughout the island, particularly in the mountains, eventually paving the way for what we now call jerk (see pages 96, 148, 159–162, and 157).

After the collapse of the Spaniards' authority on the island, much of the livestock they had introduced ran wild, including cattle and pigs. This accident only hastened the Taínos' demise. Thanks to their agricultural skill and knowledge, the Taínos' ample produce had sustained Columbus and his crew after their shipwreck on the coast of Jamaica in 1503 and 1504. Under the Spaniards, they were forced to grow vegetables, tobacco, and cotton in brutal conditions. But these and their own crops fell foul to the now-feral pigs. Before long, starvation and the violence of the Spaniards led to the deaths of all but a few of the island's original inhabitants.

Among the plants introduced to Jamaica by the Spaniards were citrus trees, including sour oranges, oranges, and lemons, as well as figs and date palms. Oviedo wrote:

> "Of the things that have been carried from Spain there can be found on the island, throughout the year, many good vegetables, many fine cattle, sweet orange and bitter orange, and very beautiful lemon and citron trees, and these fruits are to be found in abundance. There are many figs throughout the year, many date palms and other plants and trees that have been carried there from Spain."

While a wild plantain existed in the Caribbean, this was not the same as the edible plantain we speak of today. The Spaniards arrived with banana plants and, likely, plantain, of which the latter became an integral part of the island diet—especially among the enslaved people—and is still a hugely popular food today. Of the bananas' journey to the Caribbean, Oviedo wrote:

> "There are bananas throughout the year. They are not, however, native to those parts, because the first bananas were carried there from Spain. However they have multiplied so greatly that it is marvelous to see the great abundance of them on the islands... where the Christians have settled."

Over time, dishes introduced to Jamaica by different new arrivals joined forces to create entirely new dishes. Escovitch (see page 76) was introduced by Spanish Jews fleeing the Spanish Inquisition in the 16th century. Today, it remains one of the island's most enduring dishes, especially for communities living along the coastline.

Sugar cane was brought over during Columbus's second voyage, between 1493 and 1496, taken from the Canary Islands to Hispaniola, where it thrived. It was then moved throughout the Caribbean, where it found a perfect growing climate with the heat and rainfall in Jamaica. Unlike the sugar cane plantations closer to Spain, including the Canary Islands, sugar cane cultivation in Jamaica didn't need irrigation systems to be built; once planted it looked after itself until it was time to harvest. Still, the Spaniards did not cultivate it to its full commercial potential, unlike Portugal was doing at the time in Brazil.

Africans, their Food & the British in Jamaica

After the English seized Jamaica from Spain in 1655, sugar plantations were installed gradually. Other regions were turned to coffee, cotton, pimento (all-spice), and livestock, while to the East and West remained large forests. At the peak of sugar production, sugar estates made up about half of the island. There were also provision grounds, where enslaved people grew food. Their cultivation skills, honed in their homeland, were often vastly superior to that of their English enslavers; that greenfingered knowledge was vital for their survival.

Hans Sloane gave a fascinating insight to conditions in Jamaica at the end of the 17th century. He also drew detailed illustrations of plants growing in Jamaica and his writings painted vivid pictures of daily life, including the island's food and its preparation. Sloane noted that on his arrival in Jamaica in 1687, many of the plants introduced by the Spaniards were well-established:

> "This [plantain] Tree was no native to the West-Indies, but bought Thither from the Canary Isles, by one Thomas di Berlanga, a Fryar, to Santo Domingo, from whence they were sent to the other Isles and Main, and they being very useful and taking extremely, were planted every where."

Plantain was certainly "useful," not least because it was so prolific. The ease with which it flourished with little intervention would have delighted plantation owners, keen to feed their workforce as cheaply as possible: it was in their interests to ensure that their human chattels had enough energy to carry out their labors.

Hopefully, plantain offered some familiarity to the enslaved who would have known it from home. ". . . The Negroes love the Fruit," wrote Sloane, explaining how they would eat it,

> "raw, roasted, in Potage or Conserves. Plantains is the next most general support of Life in the land [after cassava]. They are brought in from the Plantain-Walk, or place where these Trees are planted, a little green; they ripen and turn yellow in the House, when, or before they are eaten. They are usually rosted, after being first cleard of their outward Skins, under the Coals. They are likewise boild in Oglio's or Pepper-Pots, and prepar'd in to a Past like Dumplins, and several other ways. A Drink is also made of them."

The versatility of plantain makes it one of the most widely used ingredients in Jamaican cooking today. Once fully grown it is tasty at any stage of its ripeness: boiled when green, fried when yellow, and baked when almost black (see pages 227, 214, and 276).

Saltfish was heavily relied upon as a protein source, as it was throughout Europe. Salted fish—predominantly mackerel, but also cod and other white fish—was imported from North America, Canada, and the seas up to Iceland. But the fish imported to the West Indies—known as West India Cure, or Jamaica Cure—was of such poor quality that it would have been universally rejected by European markets.

Chattel slavery also gave rise to the use of the "fifth quarter" in cooking, that in turn created some of Jamaica's most enduring dishes. The fifth quarter—the feet, head, tail, and entrails—would be rejected by the plantation owners and given to the enslaved workers who devised ingenious, tasty, and nutritious dishes using these scraps.

These slow-cooked dishes included stewed oxtail, cow foot (see pages 167 and 182), and mannish water, all meals that could be cooked in one pot, a cooking method favored by both indigenous and African communities.

Houses on a hill, St. Mary

The enslaved workers had to supplement their rations with foods they grew themselves on provision grounds: patches of land the plantation owners allocated for that purpose. This was not a pleasurable pursuit, but a necessity that added to the enslaved people's unimaginable burden. Hans Sloane wrote:

> "They have Saturdays in the Afternoon, and Sundays, with Christmas Holidays, Easter... and some other great Feasts allow'd them for the Culture of their own Plantations to feed themselves from Potatos, Yams, and Plantanes, etc which they Plant in Ground allow'd them by their Masters, besides a small Plantain Walk they have by themselves."

As more and more prized land was given over to sugar cane production, these provision grounds were squeezed out into increasingly inaccessible, remote areas. Foods such as plantain, dasheen, eddoes, and yams dominated the grounds. Other foods grown included beans, peas, and pulses. Rice was rare; the processing of it proved too time-consuming to be more widely cultivated. Hans Sloane, again:

> "Rice is here planted by some Negros in their own Plantations, and thrives well, but because it requires much beating, and a particular Art to separate the Grain from the Husk, 'tis thought too troublesom for its price, and so neglected by most Planters."

The pairing of rice and peas—either pigeon peas or red peas (kidney beans)—is said to have originated around the 17th century and is likely to have its roots in *waakye*, a dish from what is now Ghana.

Coffee was brought to the island around 1728 by Jamaica's governor, Sir Nicholas Lawes. A single Arabica was planted at his property in St. Andrews, where it soon spread throughout the foothills and then up the Blue Mountains. By 1737, a law passed in England reducing the tax paid on coffee imports saw almost 40 tonnes of coffee exported by Jamaica. Today, Blue Mountain coffee is one of the most sought-after in the world.

The slave trade routes that dealt in human cargo also brought new plants from Africa to the Caribbean. Seeds of the ackee tree, whose fruit is eaten as a vegetable and is as synonymous with Jamaica as reggae music, made their way to the Americas, perhaps as necklaces worn by Africans as talismans. Officially, they were introduced to Jamaica on a slave ship from Africa in 1778 and recorded in a catalog (*Hortus Eastensis*) of the exotic plants found in the garden of the West Indian-born slave-owner Hinton East in 1794. It reads like a shopping list of everything growing in Jamaica by the end of the 18th century, and, "As far as can be ascertained, the epoch of their introduction." In it, ackee is written as "akee", derived from Ghana's Twi language where it is known as ankye: "This plant was brought here in a Slave Ship from the Coast of Africa, and now grows very luxuriant, producing every year very large quantities of fruit; several gentlemen are now encouraging the propagation of it."

The pairing of ackee with saltfish made it famous, and this perfect culinary partnership is likely to have occurred soon after the ackee tree became established on the island.

Yam and okra also arrived on the slave ships. Mango first arrived in 1782, from "the East Indies" via a French ship bound for Hispaniola. The Captain also brought "many other plants and seeds and sent as a prize to this island," which could have included spices such as turmeric, galangal, arrowroot, and common ginger, which were all growing in Hinton East's vast gardens, as well as Guinea pepper, better known today as the commonly used West African spice Grains of Paradise. These seeds of *Aframomum melegueta* look like peppercorns and have a light, peppery heat with notes of cardamom, coriander, citrus, ginger, nutmeg, and juniper. It is used widely throughout West Africa in spice rubs and braises as well as in sweet dishes. There was also cumin, tamarind, black pepper, sorrel (hibiscus), and different types of sage.

The botanical garden at Bath, in St. Thomas, established in 1779, housed many new plant species; it even served as a nursery to propagate those selected for further planting throughout the island. Most notably, it is where the first breadfruit was successfully grown, after sixty-six plants "in the finest order" were brought from Tahiti by Captain William Bligh. (Bligh famously survived a mutiny on his ship Bounty during his first attempt to bring breadfruit and other plants to the Caribbean, surviving forty-eight days on a lifeboat with barely any rations and making it to Timor.) Today, breadfruit is a common sight throughout the island, served roasted, boiled, or roasted then fried (see page 219).

Other Jamaican culinary traditions are believed to be rooted in British food. Bun and cheese (see page 242) is believed to have originated with hot cross buns, hence their Easter connection.

Post-Slavery & the Flavors of a New People

The abolition of the slave trade in 1807 and the end of chattel slavery in 1833 paved the way for a new type of cheap labor: indentured workers from India and China.

While many spices were already grown in Jamaica, we have the Indian workers to thank for the brilliant curries that are now at the heart of island cuisine, namely curry goat and curry chicken (see pages 168 and 135). They also introduced roti to the island (see page 235).

Chinese indentured workers left their culinary legacy most notably in the form of soy sauce, which is often added as an ingredient in jerk marinades.

Jamaican Food: A Legacy

Together, the indigenous Taíno and, later, the enslaved people from Central and West Africa, created a legacy cuisine that drew on new and old, both in terms of influences and ingredients. I wish they had been given the opportunity to record their own thoughts and their own stories, rather than the bulk of their history being told only through records written by white Europeans.

What would our Jamaican ancestors make of those dishes still being made today? Would they laugh that people still love saltfish, stewed oxtail, and rice and peas (see pages 167 and 231), when there are so many other choices? They would surely marvel at Jamaicans making bammy (see page 197) using a gas stove and a electric grater, though I am sure it would still taste familiar.

It saddens me that those culinary pioneers never got to have a voice. But perhaps the food *is* their voice. Their enduring legacy.

In the hills of Priory, St. Ann

PLANTAIN

Plantain was introduced to Jamaica by the Spaniards in the 16th century and became a vital food during enslavement. It formed a crucial part of the diets of enslaved people—who would have been familiar with it from their homelands—providing energy and growing with little intervention. Botanist Hans Sloane noted plantain was the second "most general support of Life in the land" after cassava bread. He also noted how they were roasted "after being first cleard of their outward Skins, under the Coals."

Similar preparations remain the most common, as the fruit's natural sweetness enables brilliant caramelization that makes them so addictive.

The secret with plantain is to take your time, as their starch needs to convert into sugars slowly. Too high a heat and they burn easily.

The classic way to cut plantain is on a slant, though if I'm cooking for a lot of people I will cut them into straight discs so they have less surface area and take up less space in the pan. My mom always just slices them in half, lengthways. Saves time!

FRIED PLANTAIN

SERVES 4 AS A SIDE

2 plantain
2 tbsp oil (vegetable, sunflower, or coconut
   oil work well), plus more if needed

Cut the ends of the plantains off and score the skins down their length, trying not to slice the fruit underneath.

Peel the plantains, then lay them on a board and cut into slices on a slant, each about ¼ in (7 mm) thick.

In a frying pan, heat the oil over medium heat and add the plantain slices, without overcrowding the pan. After a couple of minutes, reduce the heat to medium-low and cook for 10 minutes. Once they have some light browning, turn and cook on the other side. You will know they are cooked when they turn shiny, golden, and translucent rather than opaque and dull yellow.

Transfer to a plate lined with paper towels. Cook any remaining plantain, adding more oil if necessary. Ensure they are warm before serving; if the first batch have cooled too much, warm them up again in the pan.

PRESSED PLANTAIN

These are known by many names around the world: *patacones*, *tostones*, flat plantain. . . but they all taste delicious regardless of what you call them.

I used to press them with a heavy pan or my mortar and pestle after their initial cook. But at La Barra Colombian restaurant in Elephant and Castle, South London, the head chef and owner Martha showed me how to press them using a tortilla press, and I've never looked back. So if you have one, use it, otherwise stick to a heavy flat object.

Serve warm as a side to Jerk Chicken or Jerk Pork, or eat them with Avocado Salsa (see pages 148, 157, and 30).

SERVES 4 AS A SIDE

1¼ cups (300 ml) vegetable oil, plus more
   if needed
4 plantain, green but starting to ripen
sea salt

Pour the oil into a pot and warm it over medium heat. Peel the plantain (see opposite) and cut into 1 in (3 cm) pieces (this time straight, not on a slant). Fry in the oil for 5 minutes, turning halfway if they are not fully submerged.

Line a tortilla press with a plastic bag or parchment paper and place a plantain piece in the middle on one of its cut sides. Cover with the other half of the plastic bag or parchment and press down, not fully, leaving the plantain about ⅛ in (4 mm) thick. Or press the pieces—again wrapped in parchment paper—under a heavy mortar or pan to the same thickness.

Repeat with all the remaining pieces.

Put 1 tablespoon oil into a frying pan over medium heat and fry the pressed plantain until golden and crispy, about 5 minutes, turning halfway. Add more oil as necessary.

Once cooked, transfer to a plate lined with paper towels and sprinkle with salt.

ROASTED BREADFRUIT

Breadfruit sits in its own category; there's nothing quite like it. Its texture is so pleasing and the flavor so delicate that it makes the perfect accompaniment to so many Jamaican dishes; it's excellent with Jerk, Stewed Oxtail, Brown Stew Chicken, Saltfish, Butter Bean & Red Pepper Stew (see pages 148, 157, 167, 145, and 79). . .

It really has to be cooked over fire. Technically, you can cook breadfruit in the oven, but it will definitely miss the smokiness that comes from it being effectively burnt on the outside.

In Jamaica, breadfruit is as inexpensive as it is plentiful. At markets on the island you can usually buy it roasted as well as uncooked, and the ashy grey of a cooked breadfruit makes them irresistible to me.

In the UK, I'll pay around £6 ($7.25) for a medium breadfruit, so it's something I reserve for when I've got a lot of people coming over. Anything left over can be warmed up or, even better, fried, which is my favorite way to have it alongside Smoked Mackerel Rundown (see page 59).

SERVES 8 AS A SIDE

1 breadfruit (3⅓–4½ lb/ 1.5–2 kg)

Light the barbecue. Cut a cross in the bottom of the breadfruit, about 4 x 4 in (10 × 10 cm).

Once the coals are ready and glowing, place the breadfruit directly onto them. Turn every 10 minutes, including so it's standing on its top and its bottom, so that it cooks evenly throughout from every direction. Continue until the surface is evenly blackened, with grey ash covering it. This will take 45–60 minutes, at the end of which the breadfruit will feel lighter.

Remove from the barbecue and wrap the breadfruit in newspaper or foil. When it is cool enough to handle, cut slices out. To serve, cut out the inner core and cut the flesh away from the ashy skin.

FRIED BREADFRUIT

SERVES 8 AS A SIDE

1 breadfruit, cooked as for Roasted
   Breadfruit (see above)
2 tbsp vegetable oil, plus more as needed
sea salt

Slice, core, and peel the breadfruit.

Heat the oil in a frying pan over medium heat and add the breadfruit. It's very absorbent, so you'll have to keep adding oil depending on how much of it you cook.

Fry for about 3 minutes on each side, until golden with browned edges. Serve with a sprinkle of sea salt.

CASSAVA FRIES WITH THYME SALT & PEPPER SAUCE MAYO

These are cooked all over the world, from South America to India and across East Africa, and the root vegetable itself has many different names depending on where you're from or where you are: yuca, tapioca, manioc... Wherever you are, the secret to good cassava fries is to boil them first, almost to the point where you think you have gone too far. The edges start to fray and the white flesh takes on a translucency. From there, once fried, the frayed edges crisp up and they are a delight to eat.

SERVES 4 AS A SIDE

1 tsp white wine vinegar, plus a splash
1 tbsp Pepper Sauce (see page 278)
1 tbsp mayonnaise
1 medium cassava (1 lb 5 oz–1 lb 10 oz/
    600–750g)
vegetable oil, for deep-frying
Thyme Salt (see page 119)
sea salt

Bring a large pot of salted water to a boil. Get a bowl of cold water ready and add the splash of vinegar.

Mix the pepper sauce, mayonnaise, and the 1 teaspoon white wine vinegar together.

Cut the cassava into sections about 2¾ in (7 cm) long. Peel the sections, ensuring the outer layer of cassava comes away as well as the brown papery skin; it should come off in a continuous roll, like a sleeve. Slice the cassava into fries no more than ¾ in (2 cm) wide, ensuring you remove the yellow-brown fibrous core running through the center of the cassava root when you get to it.

Put the cut fries into the acidulated water while you continue cutting the rest.

Once they're all cut, drain well and place immediately in the boiling water. Cook for 7–12 minutes, until the edges of the cassava begin to fray. This is important to ensure crisp fries. Drain carefully and leave to steam-dry in a single layer.

Following all the usual precautions for deep-frying (see page 288), heat the oil in a pot to 350°F (180°C); if you don't have a thermometer, dip the end of one of the fries in the oil and it should start evenly bubbling within 3 seconds. Place a wire rack over a tray lined with paper towels.

Place a batch of the fries gently in the oil, being careful not to overcrowd the pan. Fry for 7 minutes; they should be starting to color and will feel crispy against a fork. Remove with a slotted spoon and transfer to the prepared wire rack.

Repeat until all the fries are cooked, then put them in a large enough bowl to comfortably hold them. Sprinkle with thyme salt, shake the bowl to cover all the fries, then serve with the pepper sauce mayo.

FESTIVAL

A fried dumpling that's both sweet and savory? Sign me up. I adore festival and have them with everything: Grandma's Curry Chicken, Ackee & Saltfish, even Cornmeal Porridge (see pages 135, 60, and 191).

MAKES 8

2½ cups (300 g) all-purpose flour, plus
   more to dust
1 cup (150 g) fine cornmeal
1½ tsp baking powder
2 tbsp sugar
½ tsp sea salt
whole milk, as needed
vegetable oil, for deep-frying

Mix the flour, cornmeal, baking powder, sugar, and salt in a bowl and gradually add milk to bring the dough together.

Tip it out onto a lightly floured work surface and knead for 2 minutes. Then divide into 8 pieces and roll each into a small baguette shape. Place a wire rack over a tray lined with paper towels.

Pour oil into a deep pot so it's 2 in (5 cm) deep, following all the usual precautions for deep-frying (see page 288). Heat over medium heat until it is about 350°F (180°C); if you don't have an oil thermometer, a piece of the dough dropped in should first sink and then rise, bubbling after 2 seconds.

Fry the festival in batches, so as not to overcrowd the pot, for 6–8 minutes, turning until golden brown all over. Remove with a slotted spoon and transfer to the prepared wire rack to drain, then repeat the process until all the festival are cooked.

FRIED DUMPLING

Of all the dumplings in Jamaican food, fried are my favorites. During weekend breakfasts when I was growing up, Mom would be in charge of the dumpling making. Sometimes she'd sneak cumin seeds in there and wait to see if we noticed, then make us guess what she'd used. Unconventional, but tasty still.

These have the loveliest texture: chewy yet light. They're great to make with kids too, so get them involved.

MAKES 8–10

1⅔ cups (200 g) all-purpose flour
⅔ cup (100 g) fine cornmeal
2 tsp sea salt
1½ tsp baking powder
scant ½ cup (100 ml) water
vegetable oil, for shallow-frying

Mix all the dry ingredients together in a bowl. Gradually add the measured water, bringing the mixture together until it is smooth and not sticky. Leave to rest for 10 minutes.

Now take a golf ball-sized amount of dough, roll it into a ball, then squash it into a disc about 2 in (5 cm) across. Repeat to shape all the dumplings.

Heat a ½ in (1 cm) depth of oil in a frying pan over medium heat. Fry the dumplings for 6–8 minutes until they turn golden brown. Turn and repeat. Don't be tempted to increase the heat, as they burn easily and the inside won't be cooked through. Depending on the size of the frying pan, you may have to cook these in batches.

BOILED GREEN BANANAS

"Ground provisions" are starchy vegetables such as yam, cassava, dasheen, plantain, and potato (see pages 284, 282, 283, and 214). The name originates from "provision grounds," the tracts of land granted to enslaved people, where they had to grow food to supplement the meager rations provided by their enslavers.

A common way for such ground provisions to be served is as "hard food," boiled in salted water and served alongside a main dish, or in soups. These boiled bananas—as well as the boiled dumplings below—are a brilliant way to add substance to a dish, as well as mixing up the textures and flavors.

SERVES 4 AS A SIDE

2–4 green bananas
sea salt

Bring a large pot of water to a boil with a pinch of salt.

Cut the ends of the bananas off and cut each into 2–3 pieces. Add to the water and boil for 10 minutes.

Check they are tender, then remove, peel, and serve.

LORNA'S BOILED DUMPLING

Another fine recipe from Lorna Nelson, of Tranquility Estate (see page 111).

MAKES 6

1¼ cups (150 g) all-purpose flour, plus more
    to dust
3 tbsp fine cornmeal
½ tsp sea salt

Sift everything into a bowl, then pour cold water slowly into the mixture until it forms a ball.

Knead on a lightly floured surface for about 5 minutes. Split into 6 pieces, roll these into balls, then flatten each into a dumpling about 2 in (5 cm) in diameter.

Bring some water to a boil in a large pot and add the dumplings. Reduce the heat to a simmer and cook for 10 minutes, until they float (which means they're ready), then serve.

SPINNERS

Spinners are a quick and inexpensive way to add bulk and body to a soup or stew, transforming it from a snack into a meal. A couple of spinners in your dish and you'll be good to go.

SERVES 4-6 IN A STEW OR SOUP

1¼ cups (150 g) all-purpose flour
1 tsp sea salt

Place the flour and salt in a bowl and gradually add water, bringing the dough together so it is pliable but not sticky. Cover and leave it to rest for 10 minutes.

Once your soup or stew is almost ready, take a large grape-sized amount of dough and roll it between your palms, shaping it so that the ends are pointed while the middle section stays thicker.

Drop the spinners straight into the soup or stew pot, then repeat until the mixture is all used up.

Cook for 5 minutes before serving.

Making spinners with my daughter, Ada

RICE & PEAS

Rice and peas began as a Sunday staple, probably because there was more time to prepare it on the day of rest. The grain was grown by the enslaved people, though a 17th-century record states that its labor-intensity made it "too troublesome for its price, and so neglected by most Planters."

The roots of the dish are West African, born out of the Ghanaian *waakye*, a dish of rice and beans, usually black-eyed peas. Rice and peas takes its name from gungo peas, which are traditionally used, though kidney beans are fine too.

SERVES 6 AS A SIDE

scant 1 cup (150 g) dried gungo peas or
    kidney beans, soaked overnight, or a
    14 oz (400 g) can of them, with its liquid
3 scallions, finely chopped
1 garlic clove, very finely chopped
3 thyme sprigs
2 tbsp vegetable oil
1½ cups (300 g) long grain white rice, rinsed,
    then soaked for 30 minutes
1 Scotch bonnet (optional)
scant 1 cup (200 ml) coconut milk
    (for homemade, see page 271)
sea salt

In a large pot, boil the dried gungo peas or kidney beans, if using, for 1–1½ hours, until tender.

In a separate pot, fry the scallions, garlic, and thyme in the oil for 5 minutes over medium heat. Add the drained peas or beans (reserve their liquid) and the rice and stir to coat. Add the Scotch bonnet, if using, then the coconut milk. Pour in a scant ½ cup (100 ml) of beany liquid: either use the bean-cooking water or the liquid from the canned beans, making the latter up to the necessary amount with tap water.

Add a pinch of salt, but if using canned beans check whether the liquid they were in was salted, so you don't add too much.

Bring to a boil, put a lid on, and reduce the heat to a minimum. Cook for 15 minutes, then turn the heat off. Use a fork to fluff the rice up, remove the thyme sprigs if you want and the whole Scotch bonnet, if used, then clamp on the lid to continue steaming for 10 minutes before serving.

HARD DOUGH BREAD

Fresh from the Jamaican bakeries in London, to which we'd travel from Dorset to stock up on supplies, 9 bread was a precious treat to be savored. It'd be sliced and frozen, and we'd eke it out to last as long as possible, which is difficult when you're a teenager and toast and butter is a godly delight.

It took me a long time to come up with a recipe I felt was as good as my memory serves me, but this is it. It's easy to make and soon you'll be making it without having to even look at the recipe. Watching our daughter devour it like I did at her age is the best.

MAKES 1 LARGE LOAF

3¾ cups (450 g) strong white bread flour
2 tbsp sugar
¼ oz (7 g) envelope of instant yeast
½ cup (125 g) cold unsalted butter, cubed, plus more to brush the top
1 cup (220 ml) lukewarm water
1 tbsp sea salt
vegetable oil

In a large bowl, mix together the flour, sugar, and yeast. Add the butter and mix between your fingers, rubbing the butter into the flour, until there are no large lumps of butter left.

Bit by bit, pour in the measured lukewarm water: if it's too hot it'll kill the yeast and if it's too cold it won't activate it. Form a dough with your hands. It might seem sticky at first, but keep kneading and it will come together. Do not add more flour, or the dough will become too tough.

After a couple of minutes, add the salt and continue kneading, turning it out onto a work surface, until the dough is smooth, about 8 minutes. Form into a ball.

Rub the mixing bowl with a thin layer of oil. Add the dough ball and lightly rub its surface with oil so it doesn't dry out. Cover with a cloth and leave in a warm place for 45 minutes. It should double in size, or thereabouts.

Preheat the oven to 350°F (180°C).

Turn the dough out onto the work surface and "knock it back," removing the air with your fist. Flatten into a rough rectangle, roughly the width of your loaf pan and about 12 in (30 cm) long, though you will see that it finds its own size.

Starting at a shorter end, roll it up into a sausage, tucking the edges in. Do this as tightly as possible with no holes, since you don't want any air pockets in the loaf. Rub an 8½ x 4½ x 2¾ in (450 g) loaf pan with oil and, ensuring the seal on the dough is underneath, transfer it to the prepared pan. Leave to rest for 10 minutes.

Bake for 35–40 minutes until gently browned on top. Tap the bottom of the loaf and it should sound hollow. Brush the surface with a thin layer of butter.

Once cool enough to handle, turn out onto a wire rack and wait for it to cool completely before slicing.

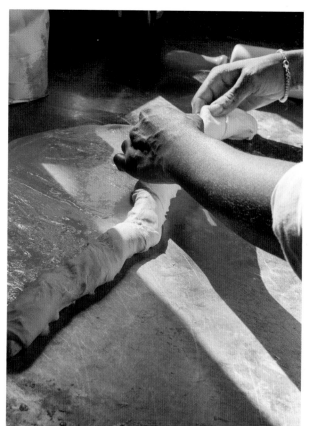

QUICK ROTI

I love roti, but I ummed and aahed about whether to include them in this book. Although they are eaten in Jamaica, they're far more widely consumed in other parts of the Caribbean, especially Trinidad and Tobago. There, "roti" often refers to meat or vegetables wrapped in a roti skin.

But I decided that they deserve a place here. Their presence in the region is thanks to the Indian indentured servants who came to Jamaica after emancipation, bringing cooking styles and dishes that were new to the area. Without that influence, there might not be roti in the West Indies.

These are beautifully buttery and flaky and well worth the effort. They are closer to what you might know as paratha, rather than the roti commonly eaten in India, which isn't flaky. There are several possible ways to make roti; this version is a quick method I started using when I became more pressed for time, but happily they still result in a delicately layered flatbread.

Served with Curry Goat or Grandma's Curry Chicken to mop up the juices (see pages 168 and 135), roti comes into its own.

MAKES 10

3¾ cups (450 g) strong white bread flour,
    plus more to dust
1 tsp sea salt
1 tsp baking powder
about 1 cup (250–280 ml) water
4 tbsp oil (canola, sunflower, or vegetable),
    plus more to oil the breads
3 tbsp unsalted butter

Put the flour, salt, and baking powder in a bowl. Make a well in the middle and add about half the measured water and 1 tablespoon of the oil. Mix well, gradually adding as much of the remaining water as you need until the dough comes together. Knead until smooth, then cover and rest for 30 minutes.

Melt the butter and remaining oil together. Lightly flour a work surface and roll the dough out to a rectangle about 24 x 16 in (60 x 40 cm). Brush it well with the butter and oil mixture and roll it up from a shorter end. Stretch the dough lengthways until you've formed a sausage.

Cut the roll into 10 pieces. Turn a piece over so it's standing spiral-end up, then press it down flat. Flatten the disc further, starting from the inside and pushing out to the edge until each is about 4¾ in (12 cm) across. Repeat to shape all the rotis, then lay them flat on the work surface and cover with a damp cloth to stop them from drying out.

Heat a frying pan over medium heat. You will cook one roti at a time. Oil the surface of a roti and cook for 3 minutes on one side, then flip and cook for 3 minutes on the other side, until both sides are golden. Keep warm under a damp tea towel as you cook the rest, then serve alongside Grandma's Curry Chicken or Curry Goat (see pages 135 and 168).

COCO BREAD

A slightly sweet, coconutty bread that is more likely to be served with savory food, coco bread is brilliant for a quick snack. Often filled with a patty—usually beef, or beef and cheese—it makes for a hearty handful that can seem insurmountable to the uninitiated. But give it a try: you'll be surprised. I like them most when I'm busy, as their clam shape makes them easy to hold with one hand while you're doing something else. And try them filled with Curry Fried Chicken, Apple Coleslaw, and Pepper Sauce, too (see pages 142, 126, and 278), or as a Plantain & Gungo Pea Bun (see page 120). A brilliant snack.

MAKES 6

1 cup (250 ml) coconut milk (for homemade, see page 271)
5½ tbsp (80 g) unsalted butter, cubed, plus 1½ tbsp (20 g) unsalted butter, melted
2½ tbsp sugar
4⅓ cups (520 g) strong white bread flour
¼ oz (7 g) envelope of instant yeast
1 tsp sea salt
a little vegetable oil

Gently heat the coconut milk and the cubed butter in a saucepan until the butter melts. Be careful that it doesn't boil. Add the sugar, stir to dissolve, then remove from the heat and wait for the milk to cool to lukewarm.

In a large bowl, mix the flour with the yeast and add the lukewarm coconut milk mixture. If it's too hot it can kill the yeast, and if it's too cool, it won't activate it. As the mixture comes together, add the salt. Turn out onto a work surface and knead until smooth, about 8 minutes.

Wipe the bowl with a thin layer of oil and return the dough, turning it to coat the top with oil. Cover with a damp tea towel and leave in a warm place to rise until doubled in size, 1–1½ hours.

Line 2 large baking sheets with parchment paper. Turn out the dough, loosely roll into a log, and cut into 6 pieces. Roll the pieces into balls, then, with a rolling pin, roll each ball into a circle about 4 in (10 cm) in diameter.

Brush the surfaces with the melted butter and fold in half to form semi-circles. Place on the prepared pans, cover with a damp tea towel once more, and leave for 15 minutes. Preheat the oven to 320°F (160°C).

Bake for 35 minutes until golden on top, then take out of the oven and leave to cool.

Something Sweet

When I think about Jamaican sweet dishes, I think of coco drops, bun, and tamarind balls. Here, I've adapted those island classics into celebratory renditions that hark back to their incredible forebears. Coco drops become a cheesecake, the ginger flavor running through its base. Tamarind is matched with chocolate for brownies.

When I'm in Jamaica, I feast on fruit that is unbeatably fresh from the tree. And in recipes such as mango and coconut panna cotta, those flavors are celebrated in recipes that bring out the fruit's best when we have to be away from the immediate abundance everywhere on the island.

BUN & CHEESE

Dad's grandad was a baker known for his bun; he worked in Clarke Castle, Richmond, St. Mary, to the North East of the island. The building that served as his bakery is still there, though most of it has been taken down and what remains—a simple blue-walled square structure—is now someone's home.

Today, bun is eaten throughout the year, but its origins lay in Easter time, in fact in hot cross buns, brought to the island by the English during the 17th century. Assimilated into Jamaican tradition, they became "bun" and took on a darker hue, with the addition of browning and molasses. The result is a beautiful, rich, spiced treat that's traditionally served with instantly recognizable orange Tastee cheese. If you can't get hold of it, mild orange Cheddar makes a close enough substitution.

MAKES 1 LOAF

⅔ cup (100 g) golden raisins or raisins
3¾ cups (450 g) all-purpose flour
1 tbsp baking powder
2 tsp ground cinnamon
2 tsp grated nutmeg
½ tsp ground pimento (allspice)
1 tsp sea salt
5½ tbsp (80 g) unsalted butter, plus
　　more to serve
½ cup (90 g) soft dark brown sugar
3 tbsp molasses
1 tbsp Sweet Browning (see page 275)
1 tsp vanilla extract
1 egg, lightly beaten
1 cup (250 ml) Guinness, or other stout
Tastee cheese and butter, to serve (optional)

Put the raisins in a heatproof bowl and pour over hot water so they are just covered. Leave for 10 minutes, then drain.

Preheat the oven to 350°F (180°C). Line an 8½ x 4½ x 2¾ in (450 g) loaf pan with parchment paper on the base and sides.

In a bowl, mix the flour, baking powder, cinnamon, nutmeg, pimento, and salt.

Melt the butter and mix in the brown sugar, molasses, Sweet Browning, and vanilla extract, then remove from the heat and, once cool, stir in the egg.

Combine the flour mix with the butter mixture until just smooth. Stir in the Guinness and drained dried fruit and mix well, then scrape the mixture into the prepared pan.

Bake in the oven for 45–60 minutes, or until a skewer inserted into the middle comes out clean.

Leave to cool before slicing and serving with Tastee cheese, or just with butter.

GRAPEFRUIT CASSAVA CAKE

Cassava has been such an important crop for Jamaica, right from the time of the Taíno to the present day. Although the diversification of available food has taken the islanders' reliance away from it as a primary food source, I think it's a brilliant vegetable, so I try to use it as much as possible.

So, this recipe is based on polenta cakes that classically call for almonds (my go-to is Nigella Lawson's lemon polenta cake). But here, instead of almonds, I use grated cassava. The result is a beautifully light cake that you'd be hard-pressed to identify as containing cassava. If you've got leftover cassava, you can make more cake batter—just multiply the rest of the ingredients—or make Cassava Fries or Bammy (see pages 220 and 197). Don't keep cut and peeled cassava in your fridge, though, as it spoils very quickly.

The best grapefruit for this is Jamaican, but if you can't get that, use pink grapefruit.

SERVES 8-10

12 oz (340 g) cassava
14 tbsp (200 g) unsalted butter, plus more (optional) for the pan
1 cup (200 g) sugar, plus more (optional) for the pan
2 tsp baking powder
finely grated zest and juice of 1 Jamaican grapefruit or pink grapefruit
1 cup (150 g) fine cornmeal
2 eggs, lightly beaten
⅔ cup (80 g) confectioners' sugar
crème fraîche, to serve (optional)

Peel the cassava, removing any discolored bits, then chop it into large chunks. Using a coarse grater, grate the chunks over a tray or large bowl, discarding the central fibrous core.

Squeeze the grated cassava between your hands. Place the squeezed-out cassava into a cheesecloth or tea towel in batches and squeeze as much liquid out as possible. Set aside.

Preheat the oven to 350°F (180°C). Line the base and sides of an 8 in (20 cm) round cake pan with parchment paper. (If your pan is made from silicone, rub it with butter, then line with a thin layer of sugar to stop it sticking and give it a nice crust.)

Using a stand mixer or electric mixer, beat the butter and sugar together until light and fluffy, about 8 minutes at medium speed.

Meanwhile, add the baking powder and grapefruit zest to the cornmeal and mix thoroughly to incorporate.

Gradually add the eggs to the butter mixture, alternating with additions of the cornmeal mixture and cassava (rub the cassava between your fingers as it goes into the bowl to break it up a bit), and allowing everything to come together before adding the next bit. This is to stop it separating.

Spoon the mixture into the prepared pan and smooth it out as much as possible. Bake for 35–40 minutes, until it's cooked through and a skewer inserted into it comes out clean.

Close to the end of baking, mix the grapefruit juice and confectioners' sugar together in a small saucepan and cook over medium-high heat for 5 minutes until it thickens slightly and is syrupy. Time this so the syrup is still hot once the cake comes out of the oven.

Using a toothpick, prick the hot cake all over and then pour over the hot syrup (you might not need to use it all, depending on how juicy the grapefruit was).

Wait until the cake has cooled slightly, then cover the cake pan with a plate and turn both upside down, then lift off the pan. Cover the cake (now on the plate) with a cooling rack and turn it again, so the cake lands gently on the rack, syrup-side up. Leave to cool. This goes nicely with crème fraîche, if you like.

COCONUT & MANGO PANNA COTTA

Panna cotta is a crowd-pleasing dessert and this combination of flavors never fails to delight. The slight tanginess of sweet mango with the creaminess of coconut is a great mixture that works in trifles and all kinds of other desserts.

This recipe will give you the ideal level of wobble, without being too stiff, and it's great for cookouts because you can make the panna cottas a day ahead and pull them out at the last minute, without breaking into a sweat.

MAKES 6

14 oz (400 ml) can of coconut milk
2 tsp unflavored gelatine powder
4 tbsp sugar
about 1¼ cups (300 ml) heavy cream
1¼ cups (300 ml) mango purée
10 ginger nut or ginger snap cookies
finely grated zest of 1 lime (optional)

Heat the coconut milk in a saucepan over medium heat until it reduces by roughly half; it will take about 30 minutes. Keep stirring occasionally to ensure it doesn't stick to the bottom and, if any lumps form, use a whisk.

Meanwhile, divide the gelatine between 2 bowls (1 teaspoon in each bowl) and cover each with 1½ tablespoons of cold water. Leave to bloom.

Once the coconut milk has reduced, stir in 3 tablespoons of the sugar and remove from the heat. Take the gelatine from one of the bowls, then add to the pan, stirring until it dissolves. Pour into a measuring jug and add enough heavy cream so you have 1⅔ cups (400 ml). Leave to cool.

Heat the mango purée in a saucepan with the remaining 1 tablespoon of sugar, adding the remaining gelatine from the other bowl, again stirring until dissolved. Remove from the heat and stir in a scant ½ cup (100 ml) heavy cream. Leave to cool.

Once the coconut and mango creams are cool, divide the coconut cream equally among 6 ramekins. Then, using a measuring jug, pour the mango cream into the ramekins in a spiral, with the spout of the jug as close to the ramekins as possible.

Refrigerate for at least 4 hours, until set.

Place the cookies in a box or sturdy bag and use the end of a rolling pin to crush them to a rough crumb (or pulse them to a crumb in a food processor). Divide the mixture among 6 plates, spreading it out thinly.

When the panna cottas are set, get a bowl of warm water and dip the base of a ramekin in for a couple of seconds to loosen the mixture. Carefully upturn it in the middle of a plate and gently tap until freed. Repeat to unmold all the panna cottas.

Grate the lime zest over the panna cottas, if you like, and serve immediately.

SORREL POACHED PEARS

This is ridiculously delicious and brilliant for those who don't drink to enjoy as a change from the more familiar French way of poaching pears in red wine. The warm spices in the sorrel (hibiscus) poaching liquid are perfect for chillier evenings, which happily coincide with pear season. As an autumnal dish, it doesn't get much better than this. You can keep the poaching liquid to use as a syrup for drinks: the spiced pear flavor is very tasty.

SERVES 4

4 pears
1 cup (250 ml) Sorrel Syrup (see page 267)
2 cups (450 ml) water
4 cloves
1 cinnamon stick
4 thyme sprigs
8 dried pimento (allspice) berries
2 tbsp dark rum (optional)
vanilla-flavored whipped cream,
    to serve (optional)

Peel the pears and slice off the bottoms to make them stand flat, but leave the stalks.

Place the pears in a pot big enough to hold them laying down, then add all the remaining ingredients.

Bring to a boil and simmer for 15–30 minutes until the pears are tender but not mushy. How long they take will depend on the variety and ripeness of the pears. Turn the pears occasionally to ensure they take on the vibrant color of the sorrel (hibiscus) evenly.

Serve with vanilla-flavored whipped cream, if you like.

The cooked pears will keep for a couple of days in the fridge, left in the liquid. You can reuse the liquid as a syrup to make drinks; it will keep for 1 month.

COCO DROP CHEESECAKE

This dish is inspired by Coco Drops, a fiery sweet that consists of chunks of coconut cooked down with sugar and a good amount of ginger; proper intense Jamaican ginger that really packs a punch. This cheesecake brings those same flavors into a dessert that stands in its own right.

SERVES 8

generous ¾ cup (100 g) dried unsweetened shredded coconut

1 ⅔ cups (100 g) coconut flakes

14 oz (400 ml) can of coconut milk

scant ½ cup (100 ml) milk

3½ oz (100 g) digestive cookies (about 7)

5 oz (150 g) ginger nut or ginger snap cookies (about 15, depending on size)

1 tbsp ground ginger

5½ tbsp (80 g) unsalted butter, melted

scant 1 cup (200 ml) heavy cream

9 oz (250 g) cream cheese

⅓ cup (80 g) soft light brown sugar

3 eggs, lightly beaten

Preheat the oven to 350°F (180°C). Line a 9 in (23 cm) springform cake pan with parchment paper.

Spread the shredded coconut out on a baking sheet and then put it in the oven for 3 minutes; do not take your eye off it, otherwise it'll burn. Move it around throughout the cooking time to ensure all of it is equally toasted. Remove from the oven. Toast the coconut flakes on a separate pan in the oven until they start to color, being careful not to burn them. Set the toasted coconut flakes aside.

Bring the coconut milk and milk to a simmer in a saucepan and add the toasted shredded coconut. Simmer for 10 minutes, then turn off the heat and let it steep for 30 minutes. Pour this toasted coconut milk through a sieve lined with cheesecloth and squeeze to remove as much liquid as possible.

Spread the spent shredded coconut on the same baking sheet as before and toast in the oven for a further 3 minutes, until it is dry. Leave to cool.

In a bowl, bash the digestive and ginger cookies until they are a fine crumb and add the ground ginger. (You can do this in a food processor.) Mix with the dried out shredded coconut and add the melted butter.

Press into the base of the prepared pan, making the edges a little higher to avoid leakage. Bake for 15 minutes, then leave to cool.

In a large bowl, whip the heavy cream until it starts to thicken. Add the cream cheese, cooled toasted coconut milk, light brown sugar, and eggs. Stir gently to avoid adding air bubbles, but if some form, just gently knock the bowl against the work surface and they should pop.

Place the pan on a baking sheet and pour in the cheesecake mixture. Transfer to the oven and bake for 50-60 minutes until the edges are set but there remains a slight wobble in the center. Remove and leave to cool.

Scatter the toasted coconut flakes on top of the cold cheesecake and serve.

GUINNESS PUNCH PIE

If you like custard tarts, you will love this. I first had the idea for it a few years ago, while drinking some Guinness punch and wondering if it would translate into dessert form. The answer was a resounding yes. The flavors work really well in a tart and you can adjust the intensity of the Guinness flavor by using slightly less or more. And if you don't drink alcohol you can use 0% Guinness: it works, I've tried.

Stout is a really popular drink in Jamaica, with Guinness and Dragon Stout cornering the market. Guinness followed the British Empire—it is also huge in Nigeria—and the company first exported a West Indian porter from Dublin to the island in 1801, with the first export of proper Guinness going out in 1830. Its long-standing history on the island is immortalized in Guinness Punch (see page 265) and this tart takes on those flavors beautifully. The slight bitterness of stout is softened by sweetness here, while the spices in the custard are really reminiscent of the stout itself. The tart makes a wonderful centerpiece, and will bring smiles of contentment to fans of the drink, as well as to everyone else.

SERVES 8

For the custard
1⅔ cups (400 ml) Guinness
7 egg yolks (freeze the whites for
    another time)
14 oz (400 g) can of condensed milk
1 cup (250 ml) heavy cream
½ tsp grated nutmeg, plus more to serve
½ tsp ground cinnamon
1 tsp vanilla extract

For the pastry
½ cup (125 g) unsalted butter, plus
    more for the pan
2 cups (250 g) all-purpose flour, plus
    more to dust
¼ cup (45 g) sugar
1 egg yolk
2 tbsp water

In a saucepan, simmer the Guinness until it reduces by about two-thirds. Leave to cool.

Meanwhile make the pastry. Using your hands, rub the butter and flour together until the mixture resembles breadcrumbs. Mix in the sugar and egg yolk and then add the measured water a little bit at a time, until the dough comes together. Don't knead any more, just wrap it in plastic wrap or parchment paper and refrigerate for 30 minutes.

Preheat the oven to 320°F (160°C). Butter an 8 in (20 cm) tart pan and remove the pastry from the fridge. Dust your work surface with flour and roll out the pastry into a circle roughly 11 in (28 cm) in diameter. Coil the pastry around the rolling pin and uncoil over the tart pan. Carefully push the pastry into the corners of the pan and leave the edges rising above the edge. Prick the base of the pan with a fork all over, then line with parchment paper and pie weights or rice. Bake in the oven for 15 minutes. Take out the parchment paper and pie weights and bake for a further 5 minutes. Remove from the oven and leave to cool.

In a bowl, gently beat the egg yolks with the condensed milk, trying not to get too much air or too many bubbles into the mixture. Stir in the heavy cream and reduced Guinness, then stir in the remaining ingredients.

Pour the custard into the pastry crust and bake for 40–45 minutes; it should still have a wobble in the middle. Remove and leave to cool.

Grate extra nutmeg over the top and chill before slicing.

COFFEE ICE CREAM

Ice cream has always been an obsession of mine. My parents bought me an ice cream maker when I was young and I experimented with loads of different flavors. Coffee was one of the earliest iterations, and it's stuck because it's so lovely. The addition of condensed milk gives a lovely familiar flavor that reminds me of my childhood, plus it works great texturally too. A secret that I considered not sharing for fear of excommunication is that I sometimes make this with decaffeinated coffee, so I can eat it in the evening without being wired all night! Look for coffee that's had the caffeine removed by water extraction, rather than by the use of solvents.

MAKES ABOUT 1¼ CUPS (300 ML) / SERVES 6

½ cup (40 g) ground coffee beans, decaffeinated if you prefer
scant 1 cup (200 ml) whole milk
scant ½ cup (100 ml) water
1 egg yolk
1 tbsp soft light brown sugar
1 tsp vanilla extract
½ tsp sea salt
scant 1 cup (200 ml) heavy cream
⅓ cup (100 g) condensed milk

Put the coffee, milk, and measured water in a saucepan. Heat until it's almost boiling, then turn off the heat and leave to steep for 1 hour.

In a bowl, whisk the egg yolk with the sugar until it is pale and creamy. Mix in the vanilla extract and salt.

Strain the coffee milk through a sieve lined with cheesecloth. If you don't have cheesecloth you can just do it through a sieve; it won't matter if there are specks of coffee in the finished ice cream.

Whisk the coffee milk into the sugar and eggs and, once all is incorporated, return to the saucepan to heat on a low temperature for 10 minutes, stirring constantly.

Remove from the heat and mix in the heavy cream and condensed milk. Transfer to a lidded plastic container and place in the freezer. Every 2 hours, use a fork to stir the mixture until it is fully frozen.

To serve, remove from the freezer for 10 minutes before scooping.

TAMARIND & BAY CARAMEL BROWNIES

Cocoa trees grow all over Jamaica and the gnarly pods, when they are in season, are a sight to behold. Once broken into, the cocoa beans are covered in an edible white pith that's delicious.

In shops you can buy balls of 100 percent pure solid chocolate which is beautifully intense, though I wouldn't recommend eating it as is. It's great for Cocoa Tea (see page 272), but also works in baking.

I've made a lot of brownies in my life, but these are my favorite. The tangy tamarind, delicately scented with bay leaves and then run through the intense chocolate, is a real treat. This recipe uses dark chocolate; get proper solid Jamaican chocolate if you can get hold of it but, if not, anything with around 70 percent cocoa solids will be brilliant.

MAKES ABOUT 16

3½ oz (100 g) tamarind, podded and deseeded (see page 279)
5 bay leaves
1⅔ cups (400 ml) water
½ cup (150 g) canned caramel (I use Carnation) or dulce de leche
5½ oz (150 g) dark chocolate (or see recipe introduction), broken up or chopped
2½ oz (70 g) milk chocolate, broken up or chopped
14 tbsp (200 g) unsalted butter, chopped, plus more for the pan
1 cup (200 g) sugar
3 large eggs
1 shot of espresso
generous ¾ cup (100 g) all-purpose flour
½ cup (40 g) cocoa powder

Put the tamarind flesh, bay leaves, and measured water in a saucepan and cook over medium-low heat for 30 minutes, until the liquid has reduced by more than half. Remove the bay leaves, then blend the tamarind into a smooth paste and mix with the caramel. Leave to cool.

Take a heatproof ceramic or glass bowl and place it over a saucepan of simmering water—being careful the base of the bowl is not touching the water—and add the chocolate and butter. Stir until melted and then mix until fully combined. (Alternatively, they can be melted in the microwave—just put the butter and chocolate in a bowl and cook for 30-second bursts until melted.) Leave to cool a little, but don't let it get cold.

In a large, separate bowl, or a stand mixer, whisk the sugar and eggs until smooth, thick, and glossy. It will take 5–8 minutes; be patient and ensure you do it properly.

Preheat the oven to 350°F (180°C). Line an 8 in (20 cm) square baking dish or brownie pan, or an equivalent-sized dish or pan, with parchment paper, sticking the paper down with smears of butter on the inside of the dish or pan.

Once the chocolate-butter mixture has cooled, mix it into the egg mixture with the espresso until fully incorporated. Mix the flour and cocoa powder together, then sift them into the wet mixture. Mix together, but not vigorously, just enough for the wet and dry mixtures to come together.

Pour into the prepared dish or pan and drizzle the caramel over the top. Use a toothpick or a skewer to swirl the caramel into the chocolate mixture.

Bake in the oven for 30 minutes. The brownie will wobble a lot when you take it out, but it's important to not lose your nerve and cook it any further otherwise it won't be gooey. Leave it to cool completely before cutting.

Drinks & Preserves

There is a perception of Jamaica as a playful nation with little seriousness. Outsiders are keen to paint it as a happy-go-lucky place, when in fact it is multi-faceted and nuanced.

But one unarguably celebratory aspect of island life is its drinks. Especially its punches, that always spell a happy time to me. Sorrel (hibiscus) is also a staple, enjoyed year round, whose complexity makes it a brilliant alcohol-free option (though it can be bolstered with a splash of rum). It also works with guava in a lovely jam. I first had guava jam when my brother Lee came home with a jar of the stuff and we worked our way through it until it was gone in a week. The sorrel in my recipe adds a new dimension to its perfumed sweetness.

The sauces in this chapter require a bit of effort, but then they're in our kitchen armory, ready to enliven many dishes from this book... or even just a bacon sandwich. Plantain ketchup is a treat and has saved me when a plantain has turned jet black and squishy in its skin. I never throw plantain away; there is always a use for it at every stage.

And I hope proper carrot juice brings as much joy to you as it did to me growing up. It was a rarity; one that I treasured.

Bar at Jack Sprat restaurant, Treasure Beach, with an array of rums

GUINNESS PUNCH

One of the most compelling drinks you can have, this is bitter and sweet and creamy all in one. Go to a jerk shop and ask for one; the mere sight of the orange-capped plastic bottle it typically comes in brings joy.

This drinks like a milkshake, but with a kick. And if the kick isn't strong enough, you can add a little rum to warm things up a bit more

SERVES ABOUT 6

1⅔ cups (400 ml) Guinness
scant 1 cup (200 ml) vanilla Nurishment
   (or a scant 1 cup/200 ml evaporated milk
   and 1 tsp vanilla extract)
½ tsp grated nutmeg
½ tsp ground cinnamon
⅓ cup (100 g) condensed milk
ice, to serve

Blend all the ingredients together. Serve with ice.

PEANUT PUNCH

Along with Guinness Punch, this is one of my favorite drinks. I love peanuts and the creaminess of this is so comforting. Peanut punch's selling point is its supposed aphrodisiac properties. It's certainly high-energy and puts anyone who drinks it in a good mood, so perhaps it's true. Recipes vary from person to person: some add Irish moss seaweed, others leave out the spices. This is mine. Feel free to add more rum.

SERVES 4

scant 1½ cups (200 g) skinned peanuts
   (or you can use ¾ cup/200 g
   peanut butter)
1⅓ cups (310 ml) condensed milk
1¼ cups (300 ml) water
½ tsp ground cinnamon
½ tsp grated nutmeg
1 tsp vanilla extract
4 fl oz (120 ml) dark rum (optional)
1 tbsp soft light brown sugar (optional)
ice, to serve (optional)

Put all the ingredients except the rum and sugar in a blender or food processor and blend until smooth. Add the rum, if using, and blend again. Taste and briefly blend in the sugar, if you want.

Serve with ice, if you like.

RUM PUNCH

Rum, a byproduct of the sugar industry, is huge throughout the Caribbean. In Jamaica its production dates back to the 17th century and it became a central part of the triangular trade route, being made on the island and transported back to Europe. It is distilled from molasses, the dark viscous liquid left after the processing of sugar cane juice.

This recipe makes a good jugful, because no one should make a single glass of rum punch.

MAKES A GOOD JUGFUL

scant 1 cup (200 ml) freshly squeezed orange juice
scant ½ cup (100 ml) pineapple juice
3½ fl oz (100 ml) dark Jamaican rum (I like Appleton Estate)
1⅔ fl oz (50 ml) white rum (I like Wray & Nephew)
juice of 3–4 limes
2 tsp grenadine syrup
1–2 dashes of Angostura bitters
¼ tsp grated nutmeg
1 tbsp dried pimento (allspice) berries
2 pineapple rings (optional)
1 small orange, sliced
1 lime, sliced
plenty of ice, to serve

Mix all the liquid ingredients together and add the nutmeg and pimento berries.

Mash the pineapple, if using, add to the liquid, and leave to steep for 20 minutes.

Add the citrus slices and ice and serve immediately.

SORREL SYRUP

There is something really festive about this drink, which comes both from its astonishing color and the aromatics. But it's brilliant all year round, warmed up on cold days, or over ice on hot days.

This will keep for a long time and is great in recipes such as Sorrel Poached Pears (see page 251), as well as when made into a vibrant jelly.

MAKES ABOUT 2 CUPS (500 ML)

2½ cups (600 ml) water
1¼ cups (50 g) dried sorrel (hibiscus)
10 cloves
1 cinnamon stick
¼ nutmeg, grated
1 in (2.5 cm) piece of ginger
1 cup (200 g) soft light brown sugar

To serve
sparkling water (optional)
lime wedges

Sterilize a 16 oz (500 ml) glass bottle, or 2 x 8 oz (250 ml) bottles or jars and their lids: Wash with hot soapy water and rinse well. Place in a pot and cover with boiling water, then boil vigorously for 10 minutes. Drain and leave the bottles or jars to cool.

Bring the measured water to a boil in a saucepan. Add all the other ingredients apart from the sugar, reduce the heat to a simmer, and leave for 5 minutes.

Turn the heat off and leave for 20 minutes. Strain, then return to the pan and set over medium heat, stirring in the sugar until dissolved.

Transfer to the sterilized bottles or jars.

Serve with still or sparkling water with lime, or with hot water. Adding a splash or so of rum is optional!

CARROT JUICE

If you've never had carrot juice, forget what you think it will taste like. And if you've ever had long-life carrot juice from a bottle or carton, don't worry: this is nothing like that. I always found those too vegetable-y and un-fresh, no doubt due to the preservation process.

As a kid, my parents would make this for us once in a blue moon and I would obsess over it, sneaking off to the fridge to take little sips and see how much I could get away with drinking before I got caught.

There are lots of versions—some call for stout, others for vanilla extract or condensed milk—but this is the carrot juice of my childhood and it requires just two ingredients: carrots and a can of Nurishment, yet the whole is so much more than the sum of its parts.

You do need a juicer for this. I asked around and managed to borrow one from a friend who had it tucked at the back of their cabinet.

When you know you're going to make this, hold on to any milk or juice bottles to store it in. Wait for it to chill first—it's so much better cold—and enjoy. I'd say it's best fresh, but in my house it doesn't hang around long enough to go bad.

MAKES ABOUT 2 QUARTS (2 LITERS)

7¾ lb (3.5 kg) carrots
½–1 can of vanilla Nurishment (or scant
   1 cup/200 ml condensed milk and 1 tsp
   vanilla extract if you can't find it)

Get a juicer, a large bowl, and enough bottles to hold about 2 quarts (2 liters)—that have been thoroughly cleaned—ready.

Rinse the carrots and remove their tops. Feed them into a juicer, ensuring its jug is in place to catch the juice, then pour into the bowl.

Add the Nurishment, stir well, and bottle. Chill and enjoy.

COCONUT MILK

Coconuts were introduced to Jamaica in the 16th century, primarily along the coast. Early records spoke of the milk in almost mystical terms, stating its superiority over dairy milk. Oviedo wrote of coconut's "excellent flavor," saying "instead of eating it, if one pounds the meat of the coconut and strains it, one gets milk which is much better and sweeter than cow's milk and of good quality." In the 19th century the coconut's production became industrialized, as coconut oil was commodified for use in cosmetics and cleaning products.

You can buy coconut milk, but making your own is lovely. You can use it in any dish that calls for it, or on its own, or as a plant-based alternative to dairy.

MAKES 2-3 CUPS (500-700 ML)

3 coconuts
2½-3⅓ cups (600-800 ml) water

Pierce each coconut through 2 of its 3 "eyes" using a skewer: be careful and *always* point the skewer tip away from you. Pour out the coconut juice into a bowl. Alternatively, you can just smash the coconut against a hard surface such as a brick wall and have a bowl ready to catch the juice. You may get some brick dust in it, but so far it hasn't hurt me.

Use a sturdy spoon to prize the flesh away from the shell. Then grate it on the finest side of a grater, or pulse in a food processor. Don't worry about the brown skin.

Put the grated coconut in a pan with the measured water; the amount depends on how thick you would like the milk to be. Warm gently until it starts to foam on top, but don't let it boil. Turn the heat off and let it steep until cool enough to handle.

Line a sieve with a cheesecloth or tightly woven tea towel (not a fluffy one) and pour the coconut milk through, then squeeze the bag until it stops dripping completely.

Transfer the coconut milk to a sterilized bottle (see page 267) and refrigerate. It'll keep for 2 days. For a richer flavor in cooking, you can use just the cream that settles on top, or shake it into the rest of the milk for other recipes and for drinks.

COCOA TEA

The first time I saw where Dad had grown up, we reconnected with his cousin Patsy. They hadn't seen each other since they were children, and it was magical.

In their yard they had cocoa beans drying in the sun, which, once ready, they would grind up and use for cocoa tea. So I dutifully picked a cocoa pod, ate all the lovely white pith that surrounds the beans, and brought them back to London. For months they sat in my warm cupboard, as I willed them to dry out, but it wasn't to be. Eventually, they went into the compost.

Thankfully, these days you can buy Jamaican chocolate online instead, if you're not in the Caribbean. It comes in balls or sticks of pure chocolate, which is ground and added to water or milk. If you can't get Jamaican chocolate, look for a chocolate that's 100 percent cocoa; specialist stores sell it, as well as some health food shops.

MAKES ABOUT 4 CUPS

1 cinnamon stick
¼ tsp grated nutmeg
2 bay leaves
⅔ cup (150 ml) water
1 chocolate ball (about 1 oz/30 g), grated into
   a powder (or see recipe introduction)
2 cups (500 ml) coconut milk (for homemade, see page 271)
brown sugar, to taste

Put the cinnamon, nutmeg, and bay in a saucepan, pour in the measured water, and bring to a boil. Reduce the heat to a simmer and leave for 15 minutes. Turn off and leave it to infuse for 30 minutes.

Bring the heat up again, add the grated chocolate, and stir until melted. Add the coconut milk and simmer for 20 minutes, stirring regularly.

Sweeten to taste and strain into cups.

GINGER BEER

An abiding memory I have of my childhood was of these little brown bottles of ginger extract that we'd bring back from London. Once home, my parents would dilute it with water, add copious amounts of sugar, heat it up, and then bottle it. It would be chilled and then we'd enjoy it. It had a punch to it, a really intense ginger flavor with hints of caramel. I loved it.

Classic ginger beer like this isn't carbonated, but you can mix the syrup with sparkling water. It also goes well with a splash of rum.

MAKES 1-1¼ CUPS (250-300 ML)

1 lb (500 g) ginger (ideally Jamaican ginger, which is thinner and more intense)
1⅔ cups (400 ml) water
1 cup (200 g) soft light brown sugar
juice of 4 limes

To serve
sparkling water (optional)
ice
lime slices

Peel the ginger with the point of a teaspoon (this is usually the easiest way, as it can peel the skin from the knobbly bits). Put it in a food processor and blend until smooth.

Put it in a saucepan with the measured water and heat for 5 minutes, but don't boil. Remove from the heat and leave it to steep overnight.

The following day strain the juice through a sieve lined with cheesecloth, squeezing out as much liquid as possible.

Put half the sugar in a saucepan and warm over medium heat until it starts to melt. Keep an eye on it and, once it starts to darken, add the strained ginger liquid and the remaining sugar. Stir until dissolved and allow the liquid to reduce slightly until it starts to thicken. Turn the heat off and add the lime juice.

Mix with still or sparkling water to taste, then serve with ice and a lime slice.

BROWNING

Browning adds depth to dishes, both sweet and savory. You can buy it, but it's easy to make and keeps for ages. A lot of store-bought browning contains salt and savory elements, so isn't good for sweet bakes.

Below are recipes for both sweet and savory browning. My savory recipe came about by accident: while making vegetable stock I over-reduced it and it became dark and intense, reminding me of browning. I added it to caramelized sugar and presto, brilliant browning! My dad swears by adding a beef stock cube or homemade beef stock to his, which you can use instead of the vegetable stock.

SWEET BROWNING

MAKES ABOUT 5 TBSP

¼ cup (50 g) soft light brown sugar
scant ½ cup (100 ml) hot water

Heat the sugar in a nonstick pot over medium-high heat until it starts to liquefy (4–6 minutes). Watch it to make sure it doesn't catch and burn.

Reduce the heat to medium-low, stirring regularly, and once the sugar has fully melted (10–15 minutes), stir continuously until it turns a luxurious dark brown and smells of intense caramel.

Add the measured water bit by bit, stirring furiously as you go. The sugar might clump up if the water is too cool, but keep it on the heat and keep stirring and the lumps will dissolve.

Once all the water has been incorporated, either use the browning straight away or transfer to a sterilized jar (see page 267). It will keep for 6 months in the fridge.

SAVORY BROWNING

MAKES ABOUT 5 TBSP

1⅔ cups (400 ml) vegetable stock
  (for homemade, see page 127)
¼ cup (50 g) soft light brown sugar

Reduce the vegetable stock in a saucepan to around scant ½ cup (100 ml), which will take about 30 minutes over medium-high heat.

At the same time, caramelize the sugar following the instructions for Sweet Browning (see above).

Once both are ready, mix together, stirring until there are no lumps. While hot, pour into a sterilized jar (see page 267) and keep in the fridge for up to 6 months.

PLANTAIN KETCHUP

I first made this after coming across a plantain so ripe its skin was completely black and dehydrated. Loath to throw it away, I tried making ketchup in the style of Filipino banana ketchup... and it works a treat. You really want plantain as ripe as possible here. If you don't have any ripe enough, bake one in the oven for an extra 20 minutes before you begin. This ketchup goes brilliantly in a bacon sandwich, or with Cassava Fries (see page 220).

MAKES ABOUT 1¼ CUPS (300 ML)

1 plantain, overripe and blackened
  (or see recipe introduction)
½ onion, finely chopped
vegetable oil
2 garlic cloves, chopped
¼ tsp ground cinnamon
¼ tsp ground pimento (allspice)
¼ tsp grated nutmeg
½ tsp sea salt
1 apple, grated
3 tbsp sugar
1 tbsp honey
3½ tbsp apple cider vinegar
1¼ cups (300 ml) water

Preheat the oven to 400°F (200°C).

Cut a couple of small slits in the plantain skin, wrap in foil, and bake in the oven for 30 minutes. Remove and leave to cool.

Sweat the onion in a splash of oil over medium heat for 8 minutes. Add the garlic, cook for 5 minutes, then add the spices and salt with a dash of water.

Once the spices are aromatic, add the cooled plantain, the apple, sugar, and honey, plus the vinegar and measured water. Cook for 20 minutes over medium heat, stirring regularly, until the water has reduced by one-third.

Blend the mixture until smooth, then transfer to a 12 oz (350 ml) sterilized glass bottle (see page 267). The ketchup will keep in the fridge for 3 months.

Jerk Chicken Gravy (in enamel jug); Plantain Ketchup (in jar with green lid and bottle with gold lid); Tamarind Brown Sauce (in jar with unscrewed gingham lid and open clip-top jar); Pepper Sauce (in plastic bottle and bottle on the right), see pages 139, 276, 279, and 278

PEPPER SAUCE

This, to me, is the ultimate hot sauce. The fruitiness of Scotch bonnets always brings something extra and, while it's hot, used sparingly it imparts brilliant flavor.

I honed this recipe for Meatopia, a live-fire food festival held annually in London. For the festival, I teamed up with Maureen Tyne (see page 182)—who serves the best Jamaican food I've had in the UK outside my family—to cook Jerk Pork (see page 157) with this Pepper Sauce. It was a winner.

MAKES ABOUT 1 CUP (250 ML)

20 Scotch bonnets
1 tbsp vegetable oil, plus more if needed
1 garlic bulb, cloves separated, peeled and chopped
1 red bell pepper, finely chopped
1 red onion, finely chopped
1 tsp dried thyme
½ tsp ground pimento (allspice)
1 tsp freshly ground black pepper
½ tsp ground cinnamon
1½ tsp sea salt
scant ½ cup (100 ml) apple cider vinegar
⅔ cup (150 ml) water
2 tbsp sugar

Wearing food-safe plastic gloves, de-stem the Scotch bonnets and remove the seeds, unless you want the sauce to be extremely hot. Don't try to do this with your bare hands.

Heat the oil in a large pot over medium-low heat and add the Scotch bonnets, garlic, red pepper, and red onion. Sweat out for 10 minutes without coloring.

Then add the thyme, pimento, pepper, cinnamon, and salt and cook for another 5 minutes. Add a splash more oil to loosen, if needed.

Add the remaining ingredients, bring to a boil, then reduce the heat to a simmer. Cook for 1 hour.

Blend to your desired consistency, pour into sterilized glass containers (see page 267), let cool, and cover. It will keep for 3 months in the fridge.

TAMARIND BROWN SAUCE

This sauce is really versatile. It's sweet but tangy thanks to the tamarind and works well as a sauce in a breakfast sandwich, on the side of a plate of food in place of ketchup, with Cassava Fries (see page 220) or regular fries, or as a barbecue sauce for meat or vegetables. You can find tamarind pods in stores and markets selling Caribbean or African ingredients, or in Middle Eastern and South Asian stores. If all else fails, you can buy them online.

MAKES ABOUT 3 CUPS (750 ML)

14 oz (400 g) tamarind pods
1⅔ cups (400 ml) water
1 onion, finely chopped
1 tbsp vegetable oil
3 garlic cloves, crushed
1 in (2.5 cm) piece of ginger, finely grated
1 apple, finely chopped
2 tsp sea salt
½ tsp ground cinnamon
½ tsp ground pimento (allspice)
3½ tbsp apple cider vinegar
scant ½ cup (100 ml) ketchup
1 tsp Worcestershire sauce, or a vegan
   version such as Henderson's Relish,
   if you need this to be vegan
½ cup (100 g) soft light brown sugar
1 tbsp molasses, black treacle, or Sweet
   Browning (see page 275)

Pod and deseed the tamarind, removing any stringy bits, and place the pulp in a saucepan with the measured water. Bring to a boil, then reduce the heat to a simmer and cook for 20 minutes, stirring occasionally. Turn the heat off and leave to rest. Once cool, puree using a food processor or stick blender.

In another pot, fry the onion in the oil for 5 minutes until soft. Add the garlic, ginger, apple, salt, and spices and cook for a further 5 minutes. Pour in the vinegar, ketchup, and tamarind pulp, Worcestershire sauce, light brown sugar, and molasses, treacle, or Sweet Browning and cook the sauce for 30 minutes over medium-low heat.

Blend the whole mixture again until smooth and strain through a regular sieve, not a fine one. Use the back of a ladle to push the liquid through so only the thickest pulp remains in the sieve. When hot, the sauce should be quite runny; it will thicken as it cools. If it looks too thick, add a little bit more water, warm it so it just starts bubbling. If it's too thin, return to the heat and stir constantly until it thickens.

Pour into sterilized jars (see page 167), cover, and label. It will last for 3 months in the fridge and is best left for a week before opening.

GUAVA & SORREL JAM

I remember my brother excitedly handing me a jar of "guava jelly," as it was labeled: I tasted it and I thought it was incredible. I love making jam and preserving vegetables and I have been lucky enough to get hold of some guava on the edge of over-ripeness for a really good price. They're perfect for this jam, which I once experimented with by adding a little of my Sorrel Syrup (see page 269), and it was beautiful. You can omit that if you choose and go for straight guava jam, but the syrup adds a lovely flavorful kick. Have it on toast, or with cake.

MAKES 2³/₄-3¹/₃ CUPS (650-800 ML)

2 cups (500 ml) water
1 lb (500 g) guava, peeled and roughly
   chopped
scant ½ cup (100 ml) Sorrel Syrup (optional,
   see page 267)
2½ cups (500 g) brown sugar
juice of 1 lemon

Pour the measured water into a pot, add the guava, and cook until the guava is falling apart. Tip it all into a blender, blend, then push as much of the fruit through a sieve as possible to remove the seeds.

Return to the pot with the Sorrel Syrup, if using, sugar, and lemon juice and cook for 30–50 minutes until the jam has thickened to the desired consistency, remembering that it will solidify as it cools, so don't thicken it too much.

While hot, transfer to hot sterilized glass jars (see page 267) and cover. Store in the fridge.

Glossary

ACKEE

Jamaica's national fruit, ackee has two seasons on the island: January to March and June to early September. The red-skinned fruit is closed until it is ripe, when it opens up to reveal three or four creamy-yellow arils that each hold a seed. If eaten before it opens naturally, it can be toxic, due to high levels of hypoglycin A that can cause hypoglycemia. For this reason, its import into the US has been banned by the Food and Drug Administration since 1973.

Because it is so delicate, ackee does not travel well, but it is available in cans outside those countries where it grows. Though it is best known served with saltfish, ackee is also excellent in Ital dishes and in stews. When using canned ackee, always add it to dishes at the end of cooking, as it only needs warming through and prolonged time in a pot will see it break up and turn to mush.

ALL-PURPOSE SEASONING

A magic pantry ingredient that does what it says: provides seasoning for all dishes. Different brands contain varying ingredients, but they generally include pimento (allspice), celery and onion powders, ground bay and pepper, as well as cumin, coriander, and chile.

They often also contain MSG (monosodium glutamate, often listed as flavor enhancer E621), which has an undeserved bad reputation; I won't go into details here, but there is plenty of scientific evidence online to counter the widespread misinformation about MSG. What I will say is that while some brands proudly declare their all-purpose seasoning to be "MSG-free," I always choose one that does contain it. I swear it's what made Grandma's Curry Chicken (see page 135) so ridiculously good.

CALLALOO

The name of a leafy vegetable, but also the title of a dish in its own right. The leaf is the amaranth plant, though different leaves are used for the dish elsewhere. It is available fresh from Caribbean and African grocery stores, or canned. If I only had a choice of canned callaloo or fresh spinach, I'd choose big, mature, leafy spinach.

CASSAVA

A brown-skinned root vegetable with bright white flesh. Known by different names, including yuca, manioc, and tapioca, there are two types—sweet and bitter. Both contain toxins, though the bitter have those in far higher quantities. Eaten raw, it can be dangerous. It degrades quickly, so is often sold covered in wax to prolong its shelf life.

CHOCHO

Known elsewhere as chayote, this green-skinned vegetable is part of the gourd family. It is cooked in stews and soups as well as mashed.

COCONUT MILK

Surprisingly simple to make yourself. . . check out the recipe on page 271. But if you want to buy it, look for a brand that has at least 10 percent fat content, as it will be creamier. Jamaica Valley, KTC, and Tropical Sun are all good brands.

Coconut milk for drinking isn't the same. It's often mixed with other ingredients such as rice, so the flavor isn't as intense. (Though I did once use it when I'd run out of canned coconut milk, and it was better than nothing.)

Growing up we used creamed coconut; blocks of solid coconut that you melt into dishes. Nowadays I much prefer cans, though creamed coconut is always good to have on hand as a back-up as it lasts for ages.

COCOYAM

A relative of regular yam, cocoyam is smaller and has distinguishable lines that run around the brown hairy skin. It can be used in the same way as regular yam.

CORNMEAL

Cornmeal is dried and ground corn, with varying degrees of texture from fine to coarse. It's made from maize, of a different variety to the sweet corn that's typically eaten straight from the cob. Try to buy the correct stuff: although grits and polenta are also made from corn, they have different defining textures and are made from different types of corn. Cornstarch is the most finely ground, white powder, while grits and polenta are typically made from another corn variety. Caribbean, African and Middle Eastern shops will stock cornmeal, or it can easily be found online.

DASHEEN

Dasheen or "coco" looks similar to cocoyam but is generally smaller and has a nutty taste.

GUNGO PEAS

A staple of Jamaican cooking, especially in rice and peas, gungo peas are sold both dried and canned and are excellent in stews. The peas originated in India, before being transported to the African continent. Their name is believed to be derived from "Congo peas," a name given to them by the English when they came across them in Africa. From there, the peas were brought to the Americas in the 17th century during the transatlantic slave trade. They are also known as "pigeon peas" and "no-eyed peas"—to differentiate them from black-eyed peas—among many other names.

HARD FOOD & GROUND PROVISIONS

"Ground provisions" is the term for starchy vegetables such as yam, cassava, dasheen, plantain, and potato. The name originates from provision grounds, the tracts of land granted to enslaved people, where they were allowed to grow food to supplement the meager rations provided by the enslavers.

Ground provisions are commonly boiled in salted water and served with a main dish such as ackee and saltfish, or rundown. When eaten as accompaniments they are known as "hard food," sometimes even just as "food." Hard food is also cooked into soups.

OILS

In my kitchen I use good quality canola oil, coconut oil, and vegetable oil. I use canola or coconut oil for browning vegetables, depending on what I'm cooking and determined by whether the coconut taste would be welcome in the dish; if not, I stick to canola. Ideally look for deeper yellow-orange canola oils, rather than the pale "extended life" ones. For deep-frying, I use vegetable or sunflower oil. You can decant used cooking oil into a clean, dry bottle and use it once or twice more, each time straining it through a cheese-cloth-lined funnel. Always dispose of used cooking oil responsibly.

PIMENTO

Pimento, known as "allspice" in the UK and US, is a berry that grows on a tree of the same name. It's known as pimento because the Spanish settlers thought the berry was a pepper. When the English colonized Jamaica, they called it "allspice" because its scent is reminiscent of cloves, cinnamon, and nutmeg, with occasional notes of bay and even vanilla.

It is used in lots of dishes, from jerk to rice and peas and oxtail. In Jamaica, markets sell bags of berries that smell incredible. Like any spice, its potency lessens the longer it is off the tree, so often exported berries aren't as fragrant as fresh. When using the berry, smell it before use and, if it isn't giving up the most glorious combination of aromatics, add some ground cinnamon, nutmeg, and clove to the dish to give it the proper nuanced flavor. Pimento wood was traditionally used for jerk to gently smoke it and it is still used in jerk pits throughout the island. Although you can source it outside the Caribbean, it isn't a sustainable choice to import it. Instead, use bay branches and leaves to cook over, along with pimento berries soaked in water, to give a similar flavor.

SALTFISH

A staple protein during the 17th, 18th, and 19th centuries, saltfish was imported into the Caribbean and traded with other goods. Ackee and saltfish is generally made with salt cod, although other white fish is often sold as "saltfish," so check the label. Other white fish make a fine replacement, especially if the sustainability of the cod is in question.

Traditionally salted to keep for long journeys by water, the unmistakeable taste of saltfish remains its allure, even though refrigeration and freezing has made transporting fresh fish easier.

Saltfish must be rehydrated before use and the water changed several times, or it can be unpalatably salty.

SCOTCH BONNET

This is the most widely used chile in Jamaica. It is not native to the Caribbean, but believed to have traveled there from South America. Although known for its heat, the most distinctive thing about Scotch bonnets is their incredible flavor; they give dishes the most beautiful, unique taste.

Referred to as a pepper rather than a chile, if you see a dish prefaced with "pepper" then the chances are it's these and not the sweet (bell) peppers that you might expect in the US and UK. Sometimes habanero chiles are sold as "Scotch bonnets," so it's helpful to know what to look for. Scotch bonnets have a noticeable shape, with a flat rather than pointed tip, and sometimes a rounded hat-shape at the stalk end.

Often the pepper is added whole to a dish at simmering stage and then lifted out whole, so it imparts flavor without overwhelming with heat. If a milder flavor is desired, small quantities can be added without the seeds or pith, where a lot of heat is concentrated. Freeze the peppers whole and cut off bits each time, so they don't go bad.

SORREL

Sorrel comes from roselle, a flowering plant of the hibiscus family. Not to be confused with the green garden herb, Jamaican sorrel is dark red and, when soaked in liquid, releases the most beautiful bright red color and tangy, intense flavor.

Available both fresh and dried in Jamaica, it is sold dried in packages in countries where it doesn't grow. Look out for packages labeled either "sorrel" or "hibiscus."

TAMARIND

Tamarind is a pod that grows on a tree. Once ripe, the brown outer shell peels easily, revealing seeds coated in a sticky pith, which is the edible part. It has a sweet and sour, tart taste. It can be eaten as is, but is widely used in sauces and marinades, from Worcestershire sauce to soft drinks.

It is sold in different forms. The ripe pods are sold in Caribbean, South Asian, and African grocery stores, who also sometimes sell blocks of tamarind pulp that has to be soaked before use. The same stores and supermarkets often sell tamarind extract, paste, or essence, which is usually the puréed flesh ready to use. Dark, glossy concentrates are intense and last for ages. A little goes a long way.

THYME

The most widely used herb in Jamaica, added to almost all savory dishes. If possible, buy it from Caribbean or South Asian stores which will often sell the hardier variety, rather than the soft-stemmed types sold by supermarkets.

Buy several bunches, rinse them (as they can be dusty), then dry and freeze in a plastic bag that can be topped up. In recipes, I call for sprigs to be used; just throw them in whole, the leaves and softer stems will fall off and mix into the dish while the thicker stalks can be picked out before serving. One benefit of freezing thyme is that some leaves fall off the sprigs and gather at the bottom of the bag, so if a recipe calls for just leaves, such as my Thyme-Roasted Tomatoes (see page 119), you can spoon them from the bag rather than having to strip them from the stems. When a recipe calls for mixed herbs, I use thyme, rosemary, bay, and marjoram.

YAM

Brought over to Jamaica during the transatlantic slave trade, yam is both drought-resistant and prolific. A root tuber, it's eaten widely in Jamaica and the island is one of the top exporters. There are many varieties, including the most popular yellow, puna, and negro yams. They can grow to more than 3 ft (1 meter) in length, but stores sell cut tubers. Yam is great roasted, in soups, and boiled as hard food.

This page, l–r: Dutch pots, Scotch bonnets, coconut, vanilla Nurishment, yellow yam, Jamaican ginger, pimento (in higher jar), nutmeg in the shell (in lower jar), dried green seasoning, grater, Guinness, cassava, thyme, green bananas

Page 286, clockwise from top left: thyme, cassava, yam, okra, chocho, coconut, plantain, Scotch bonnets

Page 287, clockwise from top left: saltfish, Jamaican curry powder, cornmeal, pimento, nutmeg, sorrel, dried gungo peas, raw cane sugar, cocoa balls

Cooking notes

DEEP-FRYING

Of all cooking methods, deep-frying seems to strike fear into the hearts of people more than any other. It's understandable given the potential dangers of hot oil combined with a naked flame (if using gas), but it needn't be terrifying.

There are some ground rules to deep-frying safely. Never fill the pot more than halfway with oil, never leave it unattended, and heat the oil steadily rather than turning the dial up to maximum.

If you can, invest in a cooking thermometer, ideally one that has a probe for checking the internal temperature of meat or other food, as well as measuring the temperature of liquids such as oil, or sugar for caramel.

If that is not possible, drop a ½ in (1 cm) cube of bread into heated oil. At 285°F (140°C), the bread will start bubbling gently on contact and take about 5 minutes to turn golden brown. At 320°F (160°C), the bread will fizz quietly on contact with the oil and bubble more enthusiastically, turning golden after 90 seconds. At 350°F (180°C), the bread will fizz loudly on contact with the oil and turn golden brown within 30–40 seconds.

Any temperature higher than this runs the danger of what is being fried browning too quickly on the outside and not being cooked inside. If unsure, always start at a lower temperature than you think might be necessary.

DUTCH POT

A quintessential piece of Jamaican kitchen equipment, the Dutch pot—"Dutchie" for short—is an all-rounder pot made out of heavy cast iron (more commonly known as a Dutch oven in the US). It's used for a multitude of one-pot dishes, for frying and simmering. It can also be used for baking, when hot coals are placed on the lid to provide 360° heat, giving rise to the saying "Hell a top, hell a bottom, hallelujah in the middle."

Originally imported to the Caribbean from the Netherlands by Dutch traders, the pot's name stuck.

WASHING MEAT

To wash your meat, or not? I've always washed chicken before cooking it. I put it in a bowl with vinegar and cold water, give it a rub all over, drain it, rinse it, and let it dry. My dad does it, so did my grandma, and I'm sure her parents did too. Other people use lemon juice instead of vinegar, while some people clean all meat, including ground meat. I don't go that far, but I do wash poultry, as is common practice in Caribbean households as well as in other countries.

In the US and UK, the Food Standard Agency and USDA recommend not washing your meat. They suggest it runs the risk of spreading food-borne bacteria such as Campylobacter on to other surfaces. But it's easy to wash meat carefully.

There is a perception that modern hygiene standards make the washing of meat unnecessary, but if I'm buying a chicken, I want to ensure the outside hasn't been soiled during slaughter, or at any stage before it gets to my kitchen.

Stockists

When it comes to sourcing ingredients, I'm always in two minds. On one hand, I think it's important to use the correct ingredients for a dish, even if they're unfamiliar. After all, using new ingredients and learning new skills is one of the best things about cooking. That said, food is always evolving and a big part of that evolution is access to and availability of different ingredients. When they arrived in Britain in the 1950s, my grandparents would have struggled to get hold of certain ingredients, such as callaloo, ackee, and gungo peas and may have either done without, or swapped them for something similar. As long as a dish's roots are known and respected, some ingredient swaps sit fine with me.

That said, we're living in very different times to those my grandparents knew, and what we cannot get in our home towns, we can often find online.

When you're not sure where to buy ingredients to cook from this book, try any grocery store catering for South Asian, African, or Caribbean people and foods. There is often a crossover. If you can't see what you're looking for, ask and see if they can order it.

Failing that, the internet provides. These are some of my favorite stockists:

JAMAICA VALLEY

Jamaican-owned, UK-based company serving both the UK and North America. They sell grocery staples such as proper pimento (allspice), coconut milk, and sea moss, as well as spice blends including chicken seasoning. Their pimento and Scotch bonnet pepper blend is out of this world.
www.jamaicavalley.com/shop

ONE STOP CARIBBEAN SHOP

www.onestopcaribbeanshop.com

CARIBBEAN ONLINE GROCERY

www.caribbeanonlinegrocery.com

FRESH DIRECT

Fresh Direct sells all manner of fresh fruit and vegetables including cassava.
www.freshdirect.com

Bibliography

Olaudah Equiano, *The Interesting Narrative of the Life of Olaudah Equiano, or Gustavus Vassa, the African*, 1789

Hans Sloane, *A Voyage to the Islands Madera, Barbados, Nieves, S. Christophers and Jamaica*, 1707

DJR Walker, *Columbus and the Golden World of the Island Arawaks*, Ian Randle Publishers, 1992

Irving Rouse, *The Taínos: Rise and Decline of the People Who Greeted Columbus*, Yale University Press, 1992

Hilary McD Beckles, *The First Black Slave Society: Britain's Barbados 1636-1876*, The University of the West Indies Press, 2016

Clinton V Black, *The Story of Jamaica*, Collins, 1965

Bartolomé de las Casas, *History of the Indies* (translated by Andrée Collard), Harper & Row, 1971

Gonzalo Fernández de Oviedo y Valdés, *Historia General y Natural de las Indias*, José Amador de los Ríos, Real Academia de la Historia (España), 1851; Gonzalo Fernández De Oviedo (translated and edited by Sterling A Stoudemire, *Natural History of the West Indies* (Studies in the Romance Languages and Literatures Number 32), Chapel Hill, The University of North Carolina Press, 1959

JH Galloway, *The Sugar Cane Industry: An Historical Geography from Its Origins to 1914*, Cambridge University Press, 1989

Dr Jessica B Harris, *High on the Hog: A Culinary Journey from Africa to America*, Bloomsbury USA, 2011

Jerry L Mashaw & Anne U MacClintock, *Seasoned by Salt*, Sheridan House, 2007

Bryan Edwards, *The History, Civil and Commercial, of the British Colonies in the West Indies*, 1805

Walter Rodney, *How Europe Underdeveloped Africa*, Verso Books, 2018

Judith Carney, *In the Shadow of Slavery: Africa's Botanical Legacy in the Atlantic World*, University of California Press, 2011

Colleen Taylor Sen, *Curry: A Global History* (Edible), Reaktion, 2012

Karla Gottlieb, *The Mother of Us All: A History of Queen Nanny, Leader of the Windward Jamaican Maroons*, Africa World Press, 2000

James Williams, *A Narrative of Events: Since the First of August, 1834, by an Apprenticed Laborer in Jamaica* (Dover Thrift Editions: Black History), 2015

Barry Chevannes Estate, *Rastafari: Roots and Ideology (Utopianism and Communitarianism)*, Syracuse University Press, 1994

Hélène Lee, *The First Rasta: Leonard Howell and the Rise of Rastafarianism*, Lee, Chicago Review Press, 2004

Meighoo, K (1999): *Curry Goat as a Metaphor for the Indian/Jamaican Future*. Social and Economic Studies, 48(3), 43–59, http://www.jstor.org/stable/27865148

Kumar, Mukesh, and Rajani Kumari: "Indian Culture in Jamaica — Past and Present," Proceedings of the Indian History Congress, vol. 60, Indian History Congress, 1999, pp. 1027–33, http://www.jstor.org/stable/44144175

Burley, David V, et al: "Jamaican Taíno Settlement Configuration at the Time of Christopher Columbus." Latin American Antiquity, vol. 28, no. 3, Cambridge University Press, 2017, pp. 337–52, https://www.jstor.org/stable/26563976

Shepherd, Verene A "Livestock and Sugar: Aspects of Jamaica's Agricultural Development from the Late Seventeenth to the Early Nineteenth Century." The Historical Journal, vol. 34, no. 3, Cambridge University Press, 1991, pp. 627–43, http://www.jstor.org/stable/2639565

Cook, Noble David. "Sickness, Starvation, and Death in Early Hispaniola." The Journal of Interdisciplinary History, vol. 32, no. 3, The MIT Press, 2002, pp. 349–86, http://www.jstor.org/stable/3656213

Morgan, Philip D: "Slaves and Livestock in Eighteenth-Century Jamaica: Vineyard Pen, 1750-1751." The William and Mary Quarterly 52, no. 1 (1995): 47–76, https://doi.org/10.2307/2946887

Klein, Herbert S, "The English Slave Trade to Jamaica, 1782–1808." The Economic History Review 31, no. 1 (1978): 25–45, https://doi.org/10.2307/2595799

Nicholas Radburn, *Guinea Factors, Slave Sales, and the Profits of the Transatlantic Slave Trade in Late Eighteenth-Century Jamaica: The Case of John Tailyour*, The William and Mary Quarterly, Vol. 72, No. 2 (April 2015), pp. 243-286 (44 pages)

Costanzo, Angelo "The Narrative of Archibald Monteith, a Jamaican Slave." Callaloo 13, no. 1 (1990): 115–30, https://doi.org/10.2307/2931614

Morgan, Kenneth. "Remittance Procedures in the Eighteenth-Century British Slave Trade." The Business History Review, vol. 79, no. 4, 2005, pp. 715–49, https://doi.org/10.2307/25097112

Diana Lutz, *Deep History of Coconuts Decoded*: https://source.wustl.edu/2011/06/deep-history-of-coconuts-decoded/ https://runaways.gla.ac.uk/minecraft/index.php/slaves-work-on-sugar-plantations/

Plantation Life in the Caribbean, http://www.ampltd.co.uk/collections_az/plantation-life-1/description.aspx

Parry, John H "Plantation and Provision Ground: An Historical Sketch of the Introduction of Food Crops into Jamaica." Revista de Historia de América, no. 39 (1955): 1–20, http://www.jstor.org/stable/20136915

Sidney M Greenfield, *Plantations, Sugar Cane and Slavery*, Historical Reflections / Réflexions Historiques, Vol. 6, No. 1, Roots and Branches: Current Directions in Slave Studies, 1979, pp. 85-119

Sabrina R Rampersad, *Targeting the Jamaican Ostionoid*: The Blue Marlin Archaeological Project Author(s): Caribbean Quarterly, June, 2009, Vol. 55, No. 2, Caribbean Archaeology and Material Culture (June, 2009), pp. 23-41 Published by: Taylor & Francis Ltd

George E Tinker and Mark Freeland, *Thief, Slave Trader, Murderer: Christopher Columbus and Caribbean Population Decline*, Wicazo Sa Review, Vol. 23, No. 1 (Spring, 2008), pp. 25-50 (26 pages), University of Minnesota Press

Nathan Nunn and Nancy Qian, *The Columbian Exchange: A History of Disease, Food, and Ideas*, The Journal of Economic Perspectives, Vol. 24, No. 2 (Spring 2010), pp. 163-188 (26 pages), American Economic Association

Thomas, Clive Y, "Coffee Production in Jamaica." Social and Economic Studies, vol. 13, no. 1, 1964, pp. 188–217. JSTOR, www.jstor.org/stable/27853777. Accessed 12 July 2021

JH Galloway, *The Sugarcane industry: An Historical Geography from its Origins to 1914* , Cambridge University Press, 1989

A Brief History of the Caribbean, by DH Figueredo, Frank Argote-Freyre, 2008, Facts on File

Newspaper article about Richard Drax https://www.theguardian.com/world/2020/dec/12/hes-the-mp-with-the-downton-abbey-lifestyle-but-the-shadow-of-slavery-hangs-over-the-gilded-life-of-richard-drax

Michael Sivapragasam, "After the Treaties: A Social, Economic and Demographic History of Maroon Society in Jamaica, 1739–1842," PhD thesis, University of Southampton Department of History, June 2018, https://eprints.soton.ac.uk/423482/1/LIBRARY_COPY_After_The_Treaties_Final.pdf

History of the Maroons https://www.cockpitcountry.com/Maroons.html

Information about Christopher Columbus http://columbuslandfall.com/ccnav/diario.shtml

Further Reading

Slavery Background
https://www.nationalarchives.gov.uk/caribbeanhistory/slavery-negotiating-freedom.htm

Dr Jessica B. Harris, *High on the Hog: A Culinary Journey from Africa to America*, Bloomsbury USA, 2011

Slave Voyages
This website is the culmination of several groups' painstaking research to provide the most detailed quantitative information about the transatlantic slave trade. It is both fascinating and harrowing to see the vast numbers laid bare and was crucial to my research. www.slavevoyages.org

Centre for the Studies of the Legacies of British Slavery
This site has details about the enslavers of the British Caribbean, Mauritius, or the Cape at the moment of abolition in 1833, using the records of the Slave Compensation Commission. It details which owners of enslaved people were compensated, and by how much. https://www.ucl.ac.uk/lbs

Riaz Phillips, *Belly Full: Caribbean Food in the UK* (Tezeta Press, 2017) Riaz's first book provides a brilliant insight into the people who built the UK's Caribbean food scene. It's rich with history and anecdotes.

are much better when brought in firſt, than after languiſhing in thoſe Pens, for want of Food.

They infect the Blood of thoſe feeding on them, whence their Shirts are yellow, their Skin and Face of the ſame colour, and their Shirts under the Armpits ſtained prodigiouſly. This I believe may be one of the reaſons of the Complexion of our *European* Inhabitants, which is chang'd, in ſome time, from white to that of a yellowiſh colour, and which proceeds from this, as well as the Jaundies, which is common, Sea Air, *&c.*

Land-Tortles are counted more delicate Food than thoſe of the Sea, although ſmaller. They are, as I have been told, on the main Continent of *America*, pen'd and fed with Patata-ſlips, *&c.* and drawn out as occaſion requires either for victualling the Flota, or for the private expence of their Houſes.

All ſorts of Sea Tortle, except the green, are reckon'd fiſhy, and not good Food.

Manati, is taken in this Iſland, very often in calm Bays, by the *Indians*; It is reckoned extraordinary good Victuals.

Fiſh of all ſorts are here in great plenty; but care muſt be taken they be not poyſonous, this is known by the places where they uſe, where if *Manſaneel*-Apples are commonly eaten by them, they are very dangerous.

Salt-Mackarel are here a great Proviſion, eſpecially for *Negros*, who covet them extreamly in Pepper-Pots, or Oglios, *&c.*

What is uſed for Bread here, by the Inhabitants, is very different from that in *Europe* : that coming neareſt our Bread is *Caſſada*. The Root dug up is ſeparated from its outward, ſmall, thin Skin, then grated on a Wheel, or other Grater. After ſearcing, the powder is put into a Bag, and its juice ſqueez'd out, the ends of the Roots are kept for other uſes. The ſearc'd and dry *Farina*, is ſpread in the Sun to dry further, then put on a Gridiron ſet on Coals, and there bak'd as Oat-Cakes are in *Scotland*. 'Tis obſervable, that although it be a Powder when put on the hot Iron, yet preſently it ſticks together very faſt, and becomes one ſolid Cake, which being bak'd on one ſide for ſome few minutes, is turn'd and bak'd on the other almoſt as long, then put on the ſide of a Houſe to Sun. The ends of the Roots are made into a coarſer Flour, and a Bread is made of a coarſer ſort, for making a kind of Drink call'd *Perino*. The juice is poiſonous, ſo that any creature drinking of it (after ſwelling) dies preſently. But if Swine be by degrees accuſtomed to it, 'tis the moſt fatning Food that is. This juice is whiſh, and if let ſettle, has a Settlement or *Fæcule* ſubſiding, which make a very fine Flour, and this fine Flour by ſome is reckoned the beſt and moſt wholeſome *Farina*.

This

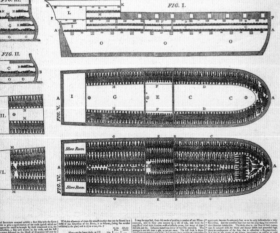

DESCRIPTION OF A SLAVE SHIP.

Top left: Extract from Hans Sloane's *A Voyage to the Islands...* (1707) in which he describes the process of "jirking" wild swine that he witnessed in Jamaica.

Top right: Olaudah Equiano, abolitionist and anti-slavery campaigner, whose autobiography *An Interesting Narrative...* (1789) gave devastating insight into the treatment of enslaved people.

Bottom left: Diagram of the Brooks slave ship (1808) showing 454 enslaved African men, women, and children shackled together. The ship sailed the triangular route from Liverpool via the Gold Coast in Africa to Jamaica. This image was made by British abolitionists to reveal the horrors of the transatlantic slave trade.

Bottom right: Taíno people grilling fish.

Above: My grandad, Altamont, arriving in Darlington from Jamaica in 1956. "Alty" is second from the right. He worked as a bus driver and he and my grandmother Catherine sent for my dad Viv once he was nine, after they had saved up enough money.

Right: My dad outside his grandfather's bakery, the first time he'd returned there since he was nine.

Acknowledgments

Motherland has been a labor of love, a balancing act of writing, research, motherhood, pandemic, and life.

But it comes after millions of men, women, and children laid the groundwork, over centuries past. We build upon their legacies and stand on their shoulders. This book is for them.

My dad Viv's magpie-like passion for foods from around the world is contagious. He's such a good cook, it's annoying. My mom's fearless in the kitchen and doesn't care about rules—she even puts cumin in fried dumpling (it works). Food was a language of love for me and my brother growing up, from plates of curry chicken waiting for us after a night out, to the lasagne we'd be sent on our way with when we left home. My parents' support, love, and enthusiasm has given me a grounding and security that has buoyed me in life and I am really thankful.

My big brother Lee makes me laugh like few people can. We used to have proper fisticuffs, but now we're too old and tired to fight, he's one of my favorite people in the whole world with a massive heart and fearless approach to life. I'm very grateful to be his sibling.

My sister-in-law Aya's *karaage* chicken first got me into cooking "professionally" and it's still the best I've ever had. I'm not sure she knows what a brilliant cook she is.

My nieces Maia and Laurenne were the best levelers during the writing of this book. They didn't care if I was on deadline and stressed; when a six- and two-year-old want to talk on the phone, you talk to them. Dianne, Marco, and Miles are the best people to eat with and introduced me to the tastiest porchetta in the world.

To my in-laws, Marie and John, Jennie, Helen, Nicki, Ben, and Ro-Ro for welcoming me into the family and buying me weirdly helpful kitchen gadgets and tasty ingredients as presents.

My agents Heather Holden-Brown and Elly James. Heather: your curiosity, humor and encyclopedic knowledge has made working with you lots of fun. I felt in safe hands navigating the alien world of publishing. It's still pretty alien, but at least we got the book out. And Elly's words of encouragement always come at the right time. She is one of the most calm and collected people.

Massive thanks to the team at Bloomsbury who took a chance on me and my idea. Rowan Yapp was the first publisher to get in touch with me and I'm thrilled we got to bring *Motherland* to life. Kitty Stogdon has been the best project editor; calm, helpful, and fun. And thanks to Maud Davies and Akua Boateng for their enthusiasm for the book and working so hard to get word about it far and wide.

Every time I look through these pages I'm reminded of what fun the photoshoot was. I love Patricia Niven's photography so much and am happy beyond words that her images are in this book. She is the loveliest, warmest, most beautiful soul, who I am blessed to call a friend.

Benjamina Ebuehi is one of the most talented people in food and to have her style this book was a dream come true. She brought out the best in the recipes while constantly making me laugh. Thank you.

Jen Kay's use of props blew my mind and made me see plants in a completely different light. If you notice an excellently placed shadow in these images, know that it's Jen, holding a plant. She is a wizard and I was in awe.

Melek Erdal helped make these recipes pop and cooks rice and peas like a Jamaican. But more than that, she is one of the most wonderful, witty, wise people I've ever met.

Massive thank you to Sam Peter Reeves, Thando Zwane, Elvira Lopez, and Sophie Bronze for helping with photography and/or babies. Cora Bird, having you on set was very special.

Anna Green's designs brought everything together in *Motherland* in the most beautiful way. From a mental image I tried to articulate she produced the most beautiful book with a cover that still sends shivers down my spine.

Thank you for your brilliant location photography Aaron Dabee, and for sticking around for an extra day so we got to watch bammy being made.

Lucy Bannell edited with intimidating eagle eyes, picking up loose ends I'd never have noticed, and being so incredibly efficient and nice along the way. Rose Davidson edited the essays with sensitivity and care, honing them from the incredibly long pieces I filed in the midst of word-blindness, into something succinct and engaging. Huge thanks to Professor Barry Higman for his expert advice.

Maureen Tyne makes the best Jamaican food in London and I'm honored she allowed me to share her cow foot recipe.

To my lovely friends. Emma W, Kirsty, Emma P, Abi, Xenia, Claire, Harriet, Cath, Ben, Hadil, Jo. The *Dorset Echo* crew who I'm forever grateful to have spent those precious three years with: Mary (so many food memories with you. Let's go cockling again), Sam, Emily, Angela, Richard, Laura, Peter, and Martin. My brilliant neighbors on "The Street," for the emergency ingredients, especially Anna & Dave for leaving all sorts on the garden wall, and for eating heroic quantities of recipe-testing food.

Thank you to my online community who support me every day, and to everyone who came to my supper clubs, pop-ups, and who has read any of my writing. Working in food has given me a brilliant community of friends. Kar Shing and Tamsin, Yvonne Maxwell, Joké Bakare, Emily Chung, Tim Anderson, Keshia Sakarah, Rachel Rumbol, Chris and Nicki, David Hall, Katy Riddle, Rav Gill, Saima Thompson (miss you), Zan Kaufman, Liam O'Keefe, Petra Barran, Chetna Makan, Asma Khan, Tiff Chan, and Angie. Special mention to Mandy Yin who once gave me priceless advice and Sarah Winman for helping me push past the mental block at the final stages.

Jaxx Nelson, thank you for Jamaica, taking me for janga soup, and never saying no to trying one last food shop. Lorna, I loved cooking with you on the veranda at Tranquility Estate and drinking that vintage rum punch. Chris and Lisa Binns of Stush in the Bush, thank you for showing me around your beautiful place and telling me your story. Thanks to Patsy, Evan, and Ruffy for allowing me to come and watch you make bammy.

Joy Francis for giving me my first proper break in journalism, Jonathan Nunn who got me to write for *Vittles* after I thought I was done with journalism. Christine Hayes, Keith Kendrick, Cassie Best, Lulu Grimes, Barney Desmazery, and the *BBC Good Food* team for getting me on board. To Tim Lusher at *The Guardian*, and Gareth Grundy and Allan Jenkins at *OFM*, for taking my words.

Thank you Lois South for showing me around the incredible collection at Liverpool's International Slavery Museum, and the staff for helping to arrange it.

A lot of my research was done at The British Library, which was then an unknown quantity to me, so thanks to the staff who made me understand how it works and to security for always being so nice. And to Dr. Polly Russell, Gary Carter, and Andrew for help with archive photography.

Mark at Swaledale Butchers: thank you for providing gorgeous meat for the book shoot. And Ruth, Nathan, Dan, Scott, and The Butchery team for the meat chats, and Oli and all the team at The Proud Sow.

And finally, to the two most precious people who light up my life. To Ada, who I look forward to seeing every morning and who puts a smile on my face every day. I love you with every bit of my being and I am blown away by the brilliant, inquisitive, funny person you are. Being your mom is a dream come true. I adore you.

And, to Kate. Thank you for giving me space to write this book and to think, as well as never questioning the state of the kitchen, and your always-honest feedback.

But it's the other things that I am most thankful for. Helping me when the sense of overwhelm grew too strong. Your brilliant mind and your unique perspective that is always 360°. For making me laugh every day and for the rare but precious times you make my tea just right. I love you more than you will ever know.

Index

About the Author

Melissa Thompson is an award-winning food writer and cook who started a supper club in her living room in London, England in 2014.

A former feature writer on a national newspaper, Melissa left newspaper journalism in 2015 to pursue her love of cooking, with her supper club growing into a sell-out pop-up across locations in London.

Born in England to a Jamaican father and Maltese mother, Melissa's food has always celebrated cuisines from around the world. She is passionate about flavor, provenance, and respecting food cultures.

As a food writer, she has penned powerful articles on the British food industry that became focal points for important discussions around identity, diversity, and inclusivity. In 2021, she won the Guild of Food Writers' Food Writing award.

This is her debut cookbook. It explores the evolution of Jamaican food, from what the island's indigenous population ate to what is known as "Jamaican food" today.

She has appeared on BBC's *Saturday Kitchen* and Radio 4's *The Kitchen Cabinet*, is co-director of the British Library's Food Season, and has chaired discussions for the event previously.

Melissa is also a columnist for *BBC Good Food* magazine and has written articles and recipes for a range of publications, including *The Guardian*, *Condé Nast Traveller*, *Stylist*, *Vittles*, *Waitrose Weekend*, *Waitrose Food,* and others.

First published in 2022 by

Interlink Books
An imprint of Interlink Publishing Group, Inc.
46 Crosby Street
Northampton, Massachusetts 01060
www.interlinkbooks.com

Published simultaneously in the UK by Bloomsbury Publishing Plc.

Library of Congress Cataloging-in-Publication Data available
ISBN 978-1-62371-801-5

10 9 8 7 6 5 4 3 2 1

Project Editor: Lucy Bannell
American Edition Editor: Leyla Moushabeck
Designer: Anna Green at Siulen Design
Photographer: Patricia Niven
Photography Assistant: Sam Reeves
Essay Editor: Rosemary Davidson
Food Stylist: Benjamina Ebuehi
Food Stylist Assistant: Melek Erdal
Prop Stylist: Jennifer Kay
Indexer: Vanessa Bird
Printed and bound in Germany by Mohn Media

MIX
Paper from
responsible sources
FSC® C011124
FSC
www.fsc.org

To find out more about our books and authors, visit www.interlinkbooks.com
and sign up for our newsletters.